Further Praise for *Leadership Lessons from the Civil War*

"As we enter the next millennium, it is imperative that we develop new management and business strategies to keep pace with our rapidly changing world. Tom Wheeler's insightful analysis of the leadership lessons of the Civil War reveals just how valuable our history can be—and how crucial it is that we learn from our past as we move into the twenty-first century."
—James A. Baker III

"A totally engrossing business 'must read.' Wheeler's nine lessons comparing Civil War strategy and leadership to modern equivalents at Coca-Cola, HBO, Microsoft, MCI, and other Fortune 50 giants is fresh and provocative . . . Demonstrates how to win in today's high stakes marketplace."
—Ivan Seidenberg
Chairman and CEO, Bell Atlantic

"It is for good reason that business is often analogized to war. This unique, thoughtful, and fun to read book proves that leadership is timeless and the lessons from over a century ago are keys to success in the competitive market of today."
—Louis W. Stern
John D. Gray Distinguished Professor of Marketing
Northwestern University
J. L. Kellogg Graduate School of Management

"Growing a business and keeping the competition in the rearview mirror requires effective leadership from every executive, manager, and project leader in the company. Tom Wheeler's *Leadership Lessons from the Civil War: Winning Strategies for Today's Managers* reveals the timeless attributes of successful leadership, as valid on Civil War front lines as on today's volatile corporate battlefields."
—James L. Barksdale, The Barksdale Group,
Former CEO of Netscape

Leadership Lessons from the Civil War

Leadership Lessons

from the

Civil War

Tom Wheeler

Winning Strategies
for Today's Managers

CURRENCY

DOUBLEDAY

New York
London
Toronto
Sydney
Auckland

A CURRENCY BOOK
PUBLISHED BY DOUBLEDAY
a division of Random House, Inc.
1540 Broadway, New York, New York 10036

CURRENCY and DOUBLEDAY are trademarks of Doubleday,
a division of Random House, Inc.

Book design by Paul Randall Mize

Library of Congress Cataloging-in-Publication Data

Wheeler, Tom (Thomas E.)
Leadership lessons from the Civil War: winning strategies for today's managers /
Tom Wheeler. — 1st ed.
     p.   cm.
Includes index.
1. Leadership.   2. Management.   I. Title.
HM1261.W48   2000
303.3′4—DC21   99-27567
CIP

ISBN 0-385-49518-8
January 2000
First Edition

10 9 8 7 6 5 4 3 2 1

For Carol, Nicole, and Max

Remembering
Raleigh M. Edgar
Charles T. Wheeler

Acknowledgments

Colonel Raleigh M. Edgar, U.S. Army (Ret.), taught his young grandson the importance of history. Before I was old enough to drive I had tromped the battlefields of the Civil War with him and listened as he made the stories come alive before my eyes.

Chuck Wheeler was a capitalist. A salesman, small on capital but large in his belief of the power and inherent good of capitalism, my father taught me to be a salesman and a capitalist by the example he set.

For years I have been drawing parallels between the lessons of the Civil War and capitalism. Those with whom I work have often been subjected to a lecture on how a current business predicament related to an example from the Civil War. One day my colleague Ron Nessen suggested I should quit talking about it and start writing.

Ron planted the seed that was fertilized by Carol Wheeler. As the wife of a man frequently made too excitable by new business ideas, Carol was also used to being dragged around Civil War battlefields. Her response to this idea was quick, decisive, and determinative, "Do it, it's in you."

Such a project is never accomplished alone. Among those to whom I am grateful for providing encouragement and assistance are: Rick Stamberger, Doug Smith, Arnold Pohs, Stan Sigman, Henry Rivera, Julian Scheer, Brian Lamb, Jerry Salemme, Bob Ratliffe, Brian Conboy, Barbara Grant, and Constantine Valhouli. Angela Rinaldi guided this rookie through the publishing world. Roger Scholl of Doubleday was both editor and guidance counselor.

Without Ron Nessen's challenge this book would not have

been started. Without his constant support and input as editor, researcher, co-conspirator, and friend, this book would not have been written. The author of many fiction and nonfiction books himself, Ron was integral in assembling this one. It wouldn't exist without him.

The blind and loving support of Carol Wheeler, Max Wheeler, and Nicole Wheeler ultimately brought forth this book. Early mornings, weekends, and vacations have been consumed by Dad's allegiance to his book project instead of to his family. They are as much a part of what is between the covers as I.

This book is the product of the inspiration, education, and support of many who have blessed me with their love, friendship, and wisdom. While my name happens to be on the cover, this is their book.

Tom Wheeler
Washington, D.C.

This Is an Interactive Book

Your input, experiences, and examples will make this book interactive and dynamic. Please visit the Web site *http://www.civilwarleadership.com* often to add your input and share in the insights and experiences of others.

To WIN TERRI, HON, MARY CHEW ...
BE PERSISTANT ...

Contents

Introduction

It came to me in the summer of 1988, when I was CEO of a small software company. Standing in front of a staff meeting, I found myself diagramming not the network we were building, but the Battle of Chancellorsville. Our company needed a bold and audacious move and Robert E. Lee's actions against the superior force of Union General Joseph Hooker in May 1863 seemed the perfect metaphor. My lifelong hobby and passion had suddenly found voice in my professional life. The battlefield strategies of Civil War generals held lessons for me—and I believe all of us—almost a century and a half later.

Early in the nineteenth century Napoleon counseled his lieutenants to study the great military campaigns of history and absorb their lessons. That advice is equally valid in business at the opening of the twenty-first century.

The history of military endeavor continues to be important for the lessons it teaches, especially the lessons about leadership. On the battlefield a leader's decisions take on a white-hot intensity, played out in full public view, with clear-cut winners and losers.

"War is capitalism with the gloves off," Tom Stoppard's protagonist observes in *Travesties*. Such being the case, the capitalist should look for lessons in the rawest form of competition. Just as Napoleon admonished his subordinates to seek out the lessons of the great campaigns, so too should business leaders learn from the experiences of battlefield leaders.

This book is for leaders at every level. One of its important lessons is that the brass on your shoulder or the title on your business card does not define leadership. A leader is anyone who has to make a decision.

In war, Union General Ulysses S. Grant observed, "anything is better than indecision." Therefore, this book is, first and foremost, a book about decision-making, organized into nine distinct lessons, each rooted in the American Civil War and practiced successfully by modern business managers.

More has been written about the Civil War than any other topic, save religion. Why? Certainly it was the greatest conflict ever waged on the North American continent, pitting brother against brother. It was the event that defined our nation and established the preeminence of Federal authority. Before the war, the common usage was "The United States *are* . . ." After the war, the newly established national unity was expressed as "The United States *is* . . ."

For me, however, the fascination of the Civil War has always been the examples of individual leadership that it provides. Leadership determines success. While there are many components in a successful undertaking (information, preparation, organization, matériel, etc.), it is leadership that is decisive, because it is leadership that harnesses all the other elements and gives them direction.

Leadership Lessons from the Civil War is based upon my belief that decisions by commanders on both sides of the Civil War provide lessons in leadership that are relevant to managers in the Information Age. This isn't a book about supermen (unfortunately, the examples from the Civil War are limited to men, since women were denied leadership roles in the 1860s). This book is about individuals who responded to great challenges with tough decisions—and what those decisions tell us about the essence of leadership. Moreover, these are the lessons that have inspired and helped me to grow both as a manager and as an individual.

The parallelisms between the challenges confronted by commanders in the Civil War and those faced by managers today are extraordinary. The war itself witnessed massive social and technological change; in the mid-1860s the United States was evolving from an agricultural society to an industrial economy, with all the associated stresses and strains. Today, a similar metamorphosis is going on as the nation evolves out of that industrial economy into a knowledge-based economy—an even more radical new structure with its own collection of stresses and strains, ambiguity, and uncertainty.

Civil War leaders were faced not only with a shift in society's tectonic plates but also with a revolution in technology that dramatically changed the conduct of war. The Civil War marked the end of the Agrarian Age, the end of Napoleonic battlefield tactics, and the beginning of modern warfare. The advent of the rifled musket, for instance, substituted a relatively precise missile for the blunt shock weapons of the past. Leadership, therefore, meant thinking anew—under pressure—and developing and utilizing new strategies and tactics to counter the advance in technology. Into this cauldron were tossed individuals yanked from civilian life who were expected to lead in battle. Some emerged as brilliant leaders; others failed miserably.

At the outbreak of the war the U.S. Army had four general officers, all of whom were of advanced age. Five years later over 1,000 men of every possible level of experience and competence had worn general's stars. In their prewar lives, these Civil War leaders were not much different in background from the business leaders of today. George McClellan was a railroad president; Joshua Lawrence Chamberlain and Thomas "Stonewall" Jackson were professors; William Tecumseh Sherman had tried banking, real estate, and teaching and was president of a small streetcar company; John S. Mosby was a lawyer; John Wilder an entrepreneur industrialist; and Ulysses S. Grant a tannery clerk. Even those who were professional soldiers, such as Robert E. Lee and John Buford, were devoid of leadership experience at this level, on this scale, or with these kinds of challenges.

There is another thread that joins the decision-makers of today with their Civil War counterparts—the uncertainty that accompanies a decision. At the time of decision no leader knows what the ultimate result will be. This book studies the decisions of both Civil War and modern business leaders as *fait accompli* with the perspective of a Monday morning quarterback. What's tough is having the courage to make the decision when the outcome rests in the balance.

When I was a young ROTC cadet we were taught there were nine principles of strategy, conveniently abbreviated as "MOSS MOUSE": Maneuver, Objective, Surprise, Simplicity, Mass, Offense, Unity of command, Security, Economy of force. Successful command decisions were the application of these nine factors.

Ultimately, however, leadership is about character and soul. I have grouped these more ephemeral attributes similarly, into nine categories, each of them offering a strategic lesson. My selection was intensely personal; as I assembled them, I learned as much about myself as I did about the Civil War. Many of the business analogies are also personal, based upon "battles" in which I participated or had an up-close view.

This is not a checklist. Every decision does not require that one utilize all nine lessons. Over time, however, each of the lessons will come into play.

No one will have difficulty recognizing my admiration of the leadership of Ulysses S. Grant. A student of military history, Grant could recite in detail all of Napoleon's campaigns and parse the decision-making that led ultimately to his defeats or victories. Yet Grant loathed war. It was the strategic aspect of war that fascinated him. The tactical application of strategy with its human carnage he found abhorrent.

In that regard, I have tried to take a Grant-like approach to the Civil War battles I describe: to study the strategic decision-making without glorifying the bloodshed. As James A. Garfield (who years later became President of the United States) wrote in describing his experience at the Battle of Shiloh in a letter to his wife:

The horrible sights that I have witnessed on this field I can never describe. No blaze of glory, that flashes around the magnificent triumphs of war, can ever atone for the unwritten and unutterable horrors of the scene.

Perhaps a modern war hero, Senator John McCain, provides the best context for these lessons: "Nothing, not the valor with which it is fought, nor the nobility of the cause it serves, can glorify war."

It is perverse that mankind's basest instinct—war—should provide the cauldron in which individuals rise and manifest some of the species' finest attributes. This book celebrates those moments when common people, placed in uncommon situations, reached into the depths of their souls and became decisive leaders. Every day, in much smaller ways in both our personal and professional lives, each of us has the same opportunity. The core challenges of leadership have not changed since the Civil War. The lessons of Civil War leaders are as current as this morning's newspaper.

Leadership Lessons from the Civil War

Lesson One
Dare to Fail

Don't confuse victory with avoiding a loss

The willingness to fail breeds success.

Decisive victories require risking a loss. A leader who fails to risk will fail to win. Of course one must consider the risks involved and avoid risk for risk's sake. But successful leaders are the leaders willing to embrace risk.

Union General George B. McClellan's fear of loss was so great that it prevented him from winning even though he commanded the most powerful force ever assembled. His Confederate adversary, Robert E. Lee, although short of troops and supplies, won his major engagements with McClellan precisely because of his willingness to risk failure.

Lee focused on the victory he could *achieve,* while McClellan focused on the loss he must *avoid.* The results demonstrated graphically that the fear of failure is too often self-fulfilling.

In a time of strategic imperative, if you don't take risks . . . you lose.

The Campaigns of 1862

Following the disastrous Union defeat at First Manassas (Bull Run) in July 1861—the first real battle of the Civil War—President Lincoln turned for leadership in the Eastern Theater to thirty-four-year-old George Brinton McClellan. Fresh from victories against Robert E. Lee in western Virginia, General McClellan was one of the few victorious officers from whom Lincoln could choose. Full of pomp, the diminutive McClellan was soon dubbed "Young Napoleon" by a press in search of heroes.

When it came to rebuilding the shattered Union army and restoring its self-respect, George McClellan was the man for the job. During the fall and winter that followed the Manassas debacle (see Lesson Four) the Union army was reorganized, and resupplied, its men drilled until they began to actually behave like competent soldiers.

McClellan seemed content to stay in camp around Washington, enjoying what he had built. "On to Richmond," however, was the cry among the media and politicians. By the spring of 1862, under intense prodding by Lincoln to go on the offensive, McClellan had devised a plan to take the Confederate capital of Richmond by striking the soft underbelly of Rebel defenses.

Most Confederate troops were concentrated between Washington and Richmond in anticipation of an overland attack. Cleverly, McClellan planned to use the Chesapeake Bay to circle around by boat, drive up the Virginia peninsula between the York and James rivers, and take the Confederate capital from behind.

Fear of Failure Stops an Army
SPOOKED AT WILLIAMSBURG

Having rebuilt a shattered Union army and conceptualized an effective plan, McClellan proceeded to squander his chance for victory.

Richmond was only a few days' march up the peninsula from where 67,000 Union troops landed on April 4, 1862. Between McClellan and the capital were only 13,000 Confederate troops commanded by Brigadier General John Magruder.

Rarely has an individual's personal traits and the military necessities coincided so well as they did with Magruder. Dubbed "Prince John," the West Point and Mexican War veteran loved high society, lived beyond his means, and reveled in pomp and circumstance. Magruder's life was an exercise in playacting—exactly the skills required by his outnumbered army. In George McClellan, the actor found the perfect audience.

Arming himself only with theatrics, Magruder took a position athwart the path of the powerful foe. Destruction of his small force seemed assured.

At the historic site of Yorktown, where George Washington received the surrender of British General Cornwallis to ensure the Revolution's success, "Prince John" Magruder made his stand. Overwhelmingly outnumbered, Magruder recast the landscape to maximize his defensive posture. One flank was anchored on a river that was dammed at key points to produce impassable artificial ponds. On his other flank, Magruder expanded the British and American trenches of 1781. With only fifteen pieces of artillery available to defend the entire thirteen-mile line, Magruder built a stage set of black-painted logs cut to look like guns.

Having recast the earth and redesigned the set to his maximum advantage, Magruder next recast his men as actors in a drama designed to convince George McClellan he was facing a formidable foe. All day long Confederate units would march among the fortifications, then circle around out of sight and march the same path again. With much whistle blowing and commotion empty trains would roll into place behind the lines, officers would shout commands at the "new troops," and buglers would blow commands. Then the engines would back up a distance, and come forward again for another noisy—and completely phony—arrival on stage.

It worked. McClellan was spooked.

Despite the reports of Rebel deserters that Magruder's army was only a skeleton force; despite reports from some brigade commanders that the line in front of them was thin; despite the fact that one probe of the Confederate line broke through (only to be ordered back); the "Young Napoleon" fell for Magruder's deception. Demonstrating his utter inability to accept risk, McClellan reasoned that a professional soldier like Magruder would never even think of holding a thirteen-mile line with only a handful of troops. Since McClellan was facing a "superior" force, he chose what seemed the most risk-free option, a siege. McClellan wrote his wife to send his books on the Crimean War siege at Sebastopol.

While McClellan hesitated, the trains on the Confederate side of the line started delivering real, not phantom, troops. By the end of April, the Confederates had almost 57,000 men on the field, augmented by thirty-six artillery batteries—real ones now, not painted logs. Magruder's goal was accomplished; McClellan had been stopped long enough for troops north of Richmond to be shifted to confront the advance.

The "Young Napoleon" wasted what the real Napoleon described as a general's greatest asset—time. It took McClellan a month to get past Yorktown, then he accomplished it only because the still outnumbered Confederate defense force, having accomplished its goal of buying time, slipped away one night and joined the now much more formidable Rebel army farther up the peninsula.

McClellan had defined his goal as *not putting his army at risk* rather than as *defeating his opponent.*

However, that did not stop McClellan from declaring victory.

"Yorktown is in our possession," his dispatch crowed the morning after the Rebels slipped away.

"Our success is brilliant," claimed a subsequent message.

McClellan's opponent, once divided and out of position, had been given time to reposition and consolidate to confront the Union force. Now numbering 80,000, the Southern troops dug into defensive positions blocking the path to the Confederate capital. Because of his inability to risk an attack at Yorktown, McClellan now faced a larger and much better prepared opponent.

Risking Failure to Achieve Victory
THE BATTLE FOR RICHMOND

Avoidance of risk continued to dominate McClellan's leadership as he marched up the peninsula. Cautiously, he brought his force—now grown to more than 100,000 troops—so close to Richmond that the Union soldiers could hear the city's church bells pealing.

There waited Confederate General Joseph Johnston. (Robert E. Lee, at the time, was military adviser to President Jefferson Davis.)

In his timid advance, McClellan had divided his force into two smaller groups, separated by the rain-swollen Chickahominy River. On May 31, 1862, General Johnston seized the opportunity to fight the Federals piecemeal. He attacked the Union troops isolated on the south side of the river in the Battle of Seven Pines.

To the cautious and deliberate mind of George McClellan such an attack was further indication the Rebels possessed vastly superior numbers. Otherwise, by McClellan's reasoning, why would Johnston take the unthinkable step of chancing a loss? In fact, McClellan continued to possess substantial numerical superiority.

There were two major casualties at the Battle of Seven Pines.

First, McClellan lost conviction in his plan. At the very gates of the Confederate capital, unable to comprehend the Rebels' strategy and unwilling to take risks himself, McClellan stopped being the aggressor and went on the defensive.

Second, General Johnston was wounded at Seven Pines. On June 1 Robert E. Lee replaced him.

Now McClellan faced an opponent whose leadership objectives were diametrically opposite to his own. For Lee, the goal was to defeat the aggressor and risk-taking was one way of multiplying the impact of his smaller force to achieve that goal. Protecting Richmond was not the *goal* but the *consequence* of attaining the goal of defeating McClellan.

A year earlier McClellan had bested Lee in smaller engagements in western Virginia. At the time he had written President Lincoln, "Lee is too cautious and weak under grave responsibility—personally brave and energetic to a fault, he yet is wanting in moral firmness when pressed by heavy responsibility & is likely to be timid & irresolute in action."

The people of Richmond shared similar concerns about their new commander. When Lee ordered the army to begin entrenching—at a time the populace wanted action—Lee was dubbed the "King of Spades."

North and South, everybody underestimated Robert E. Lee.

What Lee was doing was preparing for the offensive. First, he had to get men into the field; entrenchment strengthened Richmond's defenses, requiring fewer troops, thus allowing more men to attack. Second, Lee needed information on the enemy's dispositions—for this he turned to his twenty-nine-year-old chief of cavalry, Brigadier General J. E. B. Stuart.

Lee's orders to Stuart were risky; Stuart's implementation of the orders an even greater risk.

The young Stuart—dashingly decked out with an ostrich plume in his hat—was to take 1,200 troopers for a reconnaissance in force of the Union's right flank. Intelligence reports indicated the flank was stronger than anticipated.

Faced with a similar situation at Yorktown, McClellan had taken counsel of his fears and stopped his advance. Robert E. Lee wanted to know the facts, and was willing to risk some troops to obtain them.

Concerned about the strength of the Union force and recognizing the magnitude of what he was asking young Stuart to do, Lee worded his orders as a fatherly admonition. Stuart was, "not to unnecessarily hazard your command or to attempt what your judgment may not approve; but be content to accomplish all the good you can without feeling it necessary to obtain all that might be desired." In other words, while embracing the risk, Lee counseled his young cavalier against taking unnecessary risk.

Stuart jumped at the challenge.

"It was 2.00 on the morning of the 12th and we were fast asleep, when General Stuart's sonorous voice awakened us with the words, 'Gentlemen, in ten minutes everyone has to be in the saddle,' " one of Stuart's officers recalled. Heading north out of Richmond, the troopers (and all who were watching) thought they were on their way to join Stonewall Jackson in the Shenandoah Valley (see Lesson Five). After a fireless, noiseless bivouac that night the force surprisingly turned east into the Union flank.

On Friday the thirteenth the Rebels clashed with Federal outposts, alerting the main Union body to their existence and position. In one of the strange circumstances typical of the Civil War,

Brigadier General Philip St. George Cooke, Stuart's father-in-law, commanded the Federal cavalry response.

Despite the Union resistance, Stuart achieved his objective—he was in the rear of the Union troops with full knowledge of the strength, depth, and other details of their right flank.

"We now found ourselves in the heart of the enemy army," wrote one of the Rebel officers. McClellan's headquarters were within sight and the small force was astride the Union supply line. "Here was the turning point of the expedition," Stuart wrote in his report.

Three options faced Stuart: retrace his path and, if necessary, fight his way out; turn north and try to flank the pursuers; or go farther south, even deeper into enemy territory, and try to swing around the Federal rear. Stuart chose the latter, putting 100,000 Bluecoats between himself and the rest of Lee's army. Rain-swollen streams forced the Rebel troopers to cross at regular fords—thus setting up Union catch points—making the decision even more risky.

Stuart's officers were less than thrilled by the decision.

Clearly, Stuart loved the daring aspect of such a raid. His risky decision, however, was also logical. To return the same way he'd come would invite a collision with his pursuers, telegraph the reason for the incursion, and tip off the Federals that he'd discovered the weakness of their right flank. To move onward—while the riskiest option—would catch the Union troops off guard, wreak havoc in the rear, and mask the mission's real purpose.

Rampaging through the Union rear, Stuart attacked Federal supply docks, burning two supply ships and multiple wagons filled with stores (but not before commandeering one of the wagon's load of much needed Colt revolvers). After ambushing a troop train and causing all manner of other havoc, the troopers sought to cross the Chickahominy River and escape, only to find the bridges destroyed and the fords washed out.

A staff officer asked one of the regimental commanders, "What do you think of the situation, Colonel?" The reply: "Well, Captain, I think we are caught." Stuart thought so, too, and sent a courier to Lee requesting a diversionary assault on McClellan's front.

But a local resident told Stuart of the stone abutment remains of an old bridge. Conveniently near these supports was a warehouse that was quickly dismantled to furnish the material for a new bridge. After thirty-six hours in the saddle, thirty miles from Richmond and twenty-five miles into the Union rear, the troopers had at least put a river between themselves and their pursuers. For the first time they stopped to forage and rest.

On the morning of June 15 Stuart's cavalry trooped home through the Confederate lines, having successfully ridden completely around the Union army. They brought with them 165 prisoners, 260 mules and horses, and a reason for the beleaguered South to exult. The *Charleston Mercury* editorialized rapturously, "It is a question of whether the annals of warfare furnish so daring a deed."

Most important, Stuart brought priceless information that the Federal right flank did not extend far enough to stop what Lee was envisioning for his counterstroke. The day after Stuart's return Lee sent orders to Stonewall Jackson to bring his troops from the Shenandoah Valley to lead an assault along Stuart's path.

Ten days after Stuart's return, three weeks after taking command at Seven Pines, still badly outnumbered, Lee attacked McClellan . . . and attacked . . . and attacked . . . for seven days.

In his attack Lee continued to take risks in order to secure victory. Moving the bulk of his men away from Richmond, Lee left a significantly reduced force in the lines to defend the Confederate capital. By thus exposing his capital, Lee was able to mass a large enough force to hurl against the Union flank.

The tactic shifted the tide. Lee's risk paid off—McClellan began to retreat.

Although Lee's offensive was poorly coordinated—among other factors, the new commander and his subordinates had little experience operating together—the Confederate general pressed on. In the end, the Seven Days' Battles drove McClellan's superior force from the peninsula, onto its boats, and back to Washington.

McClellan was so worried about failure that throughout the peninsula campaign he commanded in anticipation of defeat. Immediately before Lee's first attack, McClellan had sent a telegram to Secretary of War Stanton virtually predicting defeat.

"If it [the Union army] is destroyed by overwhelming numbers," he wired, "[I] can at least die with it & share its fate."

A leader who makes decisions based on anticipation of failure will surely achieve his expectations.

By contrast, Robert E. Lee commanded without illusions but with the anticipation of victory. Lee defined his goal not as *avoiding the loss* of his capital, but as *defeating* the enemy. Outnumbered, with his back to the gates of Richmond, Robert E. Lee was willing to risk everything in the pursuit of victory.

As a result, the victory was his.

Lee's Willingness to Risk Wins Again
THE SECOND BATTLE OF MANASSAS

Lee's willingness to risk failure was not limited to his peninsula campaign.

Following the disaster on the peninsula, Abraham Lincoln faced a political problem. While George McClellan had failed, he was nonetheless a popular Democrat. To fire the "Young Napoleon" could threaten the Republican strategy that Lincoln was stitching together for the fall congressional elections. A master of such intrigue, Lincoln simply created another army and began to populate it with the returning veterans of the peninsula campaign. Soon McClellan would be a general with only a headquarters staff to command.

To command the new Army of Virginia John Pope was brought in from the west, where he had led a series of minor victories. "I have come from the west where we have always seen the backs of our enemies," the general boasted to his new command. Taking a direct shot at his predecessor, Pope further proclaimed, "I hear constantly of lines of retreat. Let us discard such ideas. Let us study the lines of retreat of our opponents and leave our own to take care of themselves. Disaster and shame are in the rear."

To prove his offensive mettle, while McClellan was still extricating himself from the peninsula, Pope moved from northern Virginia against the rail link between Richmond and its breadbasket in the Shenandoah Valley. Lee countered by sending Stonewall Jackson and 25,000 men from their positions on the peninsula.

By August it was clear to Lee that McClellan was decamping and the threat below Richmond had passed. He hurried his men north to join Jackson with the goal of defeating Pope before further reinforcements arrived from the peninsula.

Preliminary engagements convinced Pope to put the Rappahannock River between himself and Lee and to get closer to his reinforcements coming down from the Potomac. Secure in this position, Pope grew proportionally stronger each day.

Lee could not afford to let this continue.

Breaking all military maxims, Lee took the enormous risk of dividing his force in the face of superior numbers. As if that weren't daring enough, Lee planned a campaign that gave Pope the short, protected interior lines while the Rebels relied upon exposed exterior lines, with the two halves of the army beyond supporting distance of each other.

On August 25, Jackson began a sweeping left hook. Using the Bull Run Mountains as cover, Jackson's move was designed to bring him into the Union rear. Living up to their nickname the "foot cavalry," Jackson's legions moved fifty-four miles in the first two days to fall upon the Union rail link at Bristoe Station and destroy the nearby bridge over Broad Run. In one bold move Stonewall had cut Pope off from his base of supplies at Manassas Junction and put a water obstacle between his Rebel force and the Bluecoats. Then Jackson turned north, marched four miles up the Orange & Alexandria Railroad and sacked Manassas Junction with its huge stockpile of food and other supplies.

Jackson had spectacularly accomplished his goal. He was in the enemy's rear and had destroyed both supplies and transportation links. The danger required to accomplish this, however, was enormous. Jackson was now in extremis—25,000 Rebels were isolated and unsupported between two larger Federal forces. To his south Pope had 66,000 men. To his north the veterans of the peninsula were disembarking from their ships daily.

Although George McClellan was not in command of the Army of Virginia, his aversion to risk once again helped to determine the outcome. He canceled orders for his troops to be sent to reinforce Pope and close the pincer on Jackson because, "I have no means of knowing the enemy's force between Pope and ourselves." Reprising his peninsula cry that he was outnumbered, McClellan complained, "I do not see that we have force enough in hand to form a connection with Pope."

Once again the "Pseudo-Napoleon" had multiplied the strategic value of Lee's risk-taking.

As Pope turned on his heels to confront Jackson, Lee was able to send the other half of his army, under Lieutenant General James Longstreet, to follow Jackson and link up. Jackson, in the meantime, had withdrawn from Manassas Junction and was hiding under cover, awaiting the remainder of the army. Stonewall's position, along a low wooded ridge just northwest of the battlefield of First Manassas (Bull Run), was strengthened by an unfinished railroad cut, a prebuilt entrenchment from behind which his men could hold off many more than their numbers.

Jackson, however, was pathologically incapable of hiding under cover. When, on the afternoon of August 28, a Union column marched across his front, Jackson attacked. The Second Battle of Manassas was underway. For the rest of that evening and into the following day there was hell to pay as the Union forces converged to assault the Rebel position. At one point Jackson's men—out of ammunition—were reduced to throwing rocks from behind the railroad cut.

Lee's gamble, however, paid off in the nick of time. The other half of the army arrived. On the thirtieth Longstreet's men fell upon the Union flank and drove them back across Bull Run. Pope was driven back to Washington, where Lincoln relieved him of command.

Lee's grand risk-taking had succeeded once again.

Only three months before, the Union army was encamped on the doorstep of the Confederate capital. Lee's willingness to risk all, magnified by his opponents' aversion to risk, had driven the attackers out of both southern and northern Virginia.

Once again, Lee had saved the South.

Same Old Same Old
THE BATTLE OF ANTIETAM (SHARPSBURG)

Lee and McClellan would face each other a final time at the Battle of Antietam (Sharpsburg) on September 17, 1862, a mere three months after the Union retreat from Richmond and two and a half weeks from Pope's defeat at Second Manassas. It was the single bloodiest day in American history.

Now that he controlled northern Virginia, Lee had kept pressing onward. His objective was Maryland and, perhaps, beyond. Not only was he anxious to take the war onto Northern soil, Lee also believed that Marylanders, who had been prevented from joining the Confederacy as a result of some heavy-handed actions by Lincoln, would flock to his cause.

With Rebel troops across the Potomac and marching through Maryland, the fear in Washington was that Lee would flank Federal forces and fall upon the capital from the north, hitting its less heavily defended side, just as McClellan had tried to do to the Confederates at Richmond.

Lincoln had no other general to turn to but George McClellan. As before, the "Young Napoleon" had at his disposal an army that far outnumbered the Rebels.

When the Confederate capital had been threatened, Lee determined that the best defense was an offensive push to destroy the aggressor. Now, only a few months later, McClellan was in a similar position defending *his* capital. However, unlike his adversary, McClellan would not risk his position to pursue destruction of his enemy.

Once again General McClellan squandered his advantage out of fear of defeat.

Not only did McClellan outnumber Lee by almost two to one, he also had a copy of his opponent's strategic plan, accidentally left behind at a Confederate campsite (see Lesson Six). The plan indicated that Lee, once again, had divided his forces and was vulnerable to being picked off part by part. The Union general's response was to pursue Lee's scattered forces halfheartedly, in one instance delaying pursuit rather than awaken his sleeping troops.

When McClellan finally did get moving, it was the same story all over again, as the numerically inferior Confederates held off a timid Union advance at the Battle of South Mountain. The result was the same as on the Virginia peninsula—McClellan's timidity delayed his advance, telegraphed his intentions, and permitted the Confederates to rejoin their divided forces.

With McClellan advancing slowly, Lee had time to select a defensive position along a ridge outside of Sharpsburg, Maryland.

The stage was set for the bloodbath at Antietam Creek.

The Confederate line was anchored by Antietam Creek on the right and woods on the left. With the Potomac River immediately to his rear, Lee's troop disposition sent a message throughout the command—the commanding general expected victory.

After giving the Confederates an opportunity to reassemble most of their dispersed forces, the ever-wary General McClellan attacked piecemeal, permitting the Rebels to shift their outnumbered forces from one battlefield hot spot to another.

To make matters worse, McClellan repeatedly failed to rush reinforcements to those Union units that were on the brink of prevailing. At least twice McClellan's men were on the verge of breaking through Lee's lines, yet the Federal commander kept 25,000 men in reserve. Had he committed them, he would have won.

Early on the morning of the Antietam battle, Union forces attacked the left end of the Confederate line, anchored in the woods on the north end of the battlefield. For five hours the opposing armies clashed as the lines moved back and forth across a cornfield and swirled around a white clapboard church.

While McClellan failed to commit more troops to take advantage of his gains, Lee was not so restrained. Repeatedly he risked weakening one point in his line in order to pursue victory at another.

With neither side possessing a knockout punch, the action on the left of the Confederate line stalled. At that point, Union troops turned their efforts to the center.

Rebels firing from a sunken farm road, now immortalized as Bloody Lane, cut down the advancing Federals wholesale. Eventually, however, the combination of Federal firepower and numbers—as well as a mix-up that caused Confederate troops to misunderstand an officer's command as an order to retreat—enabled the Bluecoats to break the Rebel line after taking heavy losses.

If there ever was a time for McClellan to exploit a breakthrough by committing his full force, this was it. The Confederate left flank was crippled and the center had been pierced.

But, true to form, McClellan let the moment slip away. To General William Franklin, the VI Corps commander agitating for permission to advance, he replied, "It would not be prudent."

And George McClellan was eternally prudent.

As the day moved to afternoon, the action shifted to the Confederate right where a mere 450 Georgians had prevented 14,000 Union troops under General Ambrose Burnside from crossing Antietam Creek at a point now known as Burnside's Bridge (see Lesson Eight). When the crossing was finally secured, Lee's forces were again in extremis, facing fresh and numerically superior Union troops.

Again, General McClellan had an opportunity to go for victory, to decisively turn the Confederate flank and attack the exhausted Rebels in both the center and the left. But again McClellan demurred, inexplicably holding his reserves out of the battle on the safe side of the Antietam.

In distinct contrast, Lee's audacity again paid off handsomely. As the Confederate right flank was hanging in the balance, Lee saw in the distance a cloud of dust indicating the advancing troops of General A. P. Hill, the last of his disbursed forces to rejoin the main body. Their arrival allowed the Rebels to hang on.

As the day ended, Robert E. Lee had committed every last Confederate company to the battle. The Rebels essentially clung to the same positions from which they had started that morning. Lee had taken risks, had held nothing back in his pursuit of victory, and thereby had avoided destruction.

On the other side of Antietam Creek, General George McClellan sat at his command post, having failed to destroy the Rebel army because he had kept in reserve two corps of fresh, unused troops as a precaution in case they were needed after a Union defeat.

After the Civil War, McClellan rationalized holding back a quarter of his troops at Antietam: "One battle lost and all would have been lost. Lee's army might then have marched as it pleased on Washington, Baltimore, Philadelphia or New York."

By following a strategy designed to avoid losing, McClellan had assured that he would not win. McClellan had timidly fed his men into a bloody meat grinder without the will to capitalize on their sacrifice. At best, he had produced a draw.

Two weeks after the Battle of Antietam, President Lincoln visited General McClellan on the battlefield to try to convince him to advance aggressively and attack the Confederates as they moved back into Virginia. When McClellan would not pursue, Lincoln fired him.

A few months after the battle, a new national cemetery was dedicated as the final resting place for over 4,000 Union soldiers who died at Antietam. In the ultimate rebuke, the commander of those men, George Brinton McClellan, was not invited.

Emulating Lee in the Cola Wars
"CLASSIC" LEADERSHIP

In the three and a half months after Robert E. Lee took command of the Army of Northern Virginia, his undermanned and ill-supplied Confederate army had, three times, denied victory to the Union forces. Lee's willingness to risk all in the pursuit of victory is a respected business strategy as well. No one better exemplifies a willingness to take corporate risks than Roberto Goizueta when he became chairman/CEO of the Coca-Cola Company in 1981.

One of Goizueta's first acts as chairman was to convene a

meeting of Coke's top managers to discuss the company's problems in the never-ending cola wars with Pepsi, and to develop a strategy for the future. That strategy was based on what he called "intelligent, individual risk-taking."

Goizueta, a Cuban-born immigrant, often invoked the Spanish poet Antonio Machado, "Traveler, there is no path. Paths are made by walking." In other words, Coke's new boss wasn't afraid to risk treading on uncharted ground.

True to this philosophy, he made two of the riskiest decisions in American business history, daring to change one of the best-known corporate icons in the world, a century-old brand that literally symbolized America to billions of people.

Both of Goizueta's risky decisions ultimately succeeded, although one came as close to failing as Robert E. Lee had with his back to the Potomac at Antietam. Like the daring general, however, Goizueta saved the day with his willingness to redeploy and continue to risk in the face of withering opposition.

As the eighties began, Coke was still outselling Pepsi in the worldwide cola wars, by about 35 to 25 percent. But Pepsi was gaining. It was more popular with supermarket shoppers and it was the drink of choice among young people. The Pepsi Challenge TV commercials were working. Coke's own secret tests showed consumers *did* think Pepsi tasted better. And Coke's older buyers were deserting for diet soft drinks.

Goizueta could have hunkered down and clung to what he had, McClellan-style. After all, 35 percent of the world cola market produced billions in revenue. But instead of a strategy designed to avoid losing, the Coke chief boldly adopted a strategy designed to win.

First, in the summer of 1982, he introduced diet Coke in his quest to capture the loyalty of older and more weight-conscious soft-drink guzzlers.

Goizueta later said it was the toughest decision he ever made because it was the first time the company had allowed the Coke name to be attached to any drink other than the old original formula. Critics worried that diet Coke would tarnish the brand name and siphon customers away not only from Coke but also from Tab, the company's diet soft drink.

But diet Coke was a huge success, bringing millions of new customers to the Coca-Cola brand. In less than two years, diet Coke was the third-largest-selling soft drink in America. The success persuaded the company to attach the hallowed name to Cherry Coke, Caffeine-free Coke, and, most famously, New Coke.

The formula for New Coke was developed in a secret experiment, code-named Project Kansas, designed to find a taste that would appeal to a new generation of soft drink customers. It was basically diet Coke made with sugar instead of artificial sweetener—sweeter and smoother than original Coke. In 190,000 taste tests, New Coke was preferred to old Coke by 61 to 39 percent.

Goizueta decided this would be the soft drink to capture the youth market and win the Pepsi challenge. And so, in April 1985, he made the almost unimaginably risky decision to retire the ninety-nine-year-old formula for old Coke—known inside the company as Merchandise 7X—and to launch New Coke.

It would be, he predicted, "the surest thing" Coke had ever done.

It would be a fiasco. The late-night comics had a field day.

Coca-Cola was bombarded with outraged phone calls, telegrams, letters, public protests, and scorn from customers demanding their old Coke back. The new drink was ridiculed as the Edsel of the eighties. Week after week the flak continued. Pepsi was licking its chops.

"We thought the letters and phone calls would slow down," commented a Coke executive at the time. "They didn't."

Actually, the protesters were a vociferous minority. Company surveys found that 150 million Americans tried New Coke in its first ten weeks on the market, and fully 75 percent said they would buy it again.

"We're not following the lead of others," Goizueta assured anxious Coke bottlers. "We're setting the pace. We are on the front lines of change."

Nevertheless, after enduring seventy-eight days of unabated public complaints, Goizueta made yet another risky decision. The company would resume selling the old formula under the name Classic Coke while continuing to market New Coke.

"If you don't take risks, you surely will fail," Goizueta preached.

This risk was huge.

Would customers support *two* Cokes? Or would they leave the brand and go to Pepsi in confusion? How would Goizueta market two Cokes? How would he distribute them? What would the packaging look like? Could he survive a fresh barrage of mockery from the comics?

"The greatest risk of all is to do nothing," Goizueta believed. So he acted.

The strategy worked. The crisis was over.

Goizueta insisted that his chancy decision to change the Coke formula and his forced turnaround were not blunders.

"This is very much an offensive move," he maintained. "We're going to satisfy more consumers and, in the process, we're going to sell a hell of a lot more gallons of soft drink."

His statement was greeted with skepticism. Roger Enrico, then president of Pepsi-Cola USA, dashed off a book rashly and prematurely titled *The Other Guy Blinked: How Pepsi Won the Cola Wars.*

But in the end, Goizueta turned out to be right. His boldness, his risk-everything-to-win approach succeeded. Coca-Cola snatched victory from the jaws of defeat.

After the New Coke/Classic Coke controversy, combined sales of Coca-Cola's multiple products steadily pulled away from

Pepsi in both the United States and overseas. A brand loyalty survey taken two years after the New Coke upheaval ranked Coke's image among consumers at the highest level in the thirty-year history of the survey.

In fact, some cynics suggest that Goizueta deliberately cooked up the controversy, intending from the outset to reintroduce original Coke, as a brilliant publicity stunt to attract customer attention to the Coke brands and to remind them how much they loved the old flavor.

"We're not that smart," a Coke executive dismissed the suggestion. "And we're not that dumb."

An example of a company too afraid to take the calculated risk was Apple Computer in the 1980s. Because of that fear Apple lost its commanding position in the personal computer field.

Apple almost rode risk-aversity into irrelevance. Like McClellan, Apple's generals defined their objective as *not losing* control of the Macintosh operating system, instead of *winning the battle* for control of the desktop from Microsoft, Intel, and IBM. Apple executives stubbornly refused to risk licensing others to build the Mac machine, thereby limiting its market.

As once mighty Apple spiraled down to a 3 percent market share by 1996 *Forbes* commented on the company's risk-aversion strategy, "Apple is in a position where standing pat almost certainly means slow death."

The white-shirt crowd at IBM didn't do much better in the early 1980s as they followed a play-it-safe mentality to fall from the top of the computer heap. Instead of sweeping the new battlefield before it, Big Blue's entry into personal computing was designed to protect IBM's mainframe business. Producing a "crippled computer," an underpowered machine with little memory and few features, IBM set out to convince consumers they really didn't need much computing power in their desktop machine. They were blown out of the market by Compaq and other upstarts in the 1980s, which dared to define their goal as dominance of the new personal computer market through increasing power, speed, memory, and functionality.

As seen in the Civil War, it is the risk-takers in business who win the battle.

Marching Orders

Victory is not defined by *preserving* the status quo, but by *prevailing*. In business, as in battle, there can be no strategic victories without risk.

Robert E. Lee used risk as a force multiplier. Risk-averse George McClellan retired a loser despite having commanded the most powerful army ever assembled.

Apple and IBM fell from their lofty corporate perches in the 1980s because their practices were more like McClellan than Lee.

Roberto Goizueta preached a philosophy to his Coca-Cola colleagues that could have just as easily come from the mouth of the brilliantly successful Robert E. Lee: "If you take risks, you may still fail. If you do not take risks, you will surely fail. *The greatest risk of all is to do nothing.*"

It can't be stated any better.

Lesson Two

If at First You Don't Succeed . . . So What?

Tenacity

Risks result in failures. Every major decision is an invitation to defeat. But how one responds when a risk doesn't pay off can be an even greater leadership challenge than deciding to take the risk in the first place. Risk is the ante. The greater test comes when the pot is lost.

Those with the leadership skill to persevere in the face of adversity are described as "tenacious" or "persistent." Eventually, however, they are called "winners."

The Civil War produced one of the most tenacious leaders in history in Union General Ulysses S. Grant. While the war gave Grant the opportunity to leave behind a personal life dotted by failure, adversity followed him onto the battlefield.

But U. S. Grant was persistence personified. Because he refused to accept failure, he became the Civil War's most decisive—and successful—military leader.

Leadership requires the tenacity not to be undone by setbacks, coupled with the willingness to continue to take risks despite the setbacks.

For such leaders, failure is only an interim step on the path to success.

Grant

Ulysses S. Grant was the polar opposite of Robert E. Lee. The poor country boy from the west and the to-the-manor-born aristocrat from the south had only West Point and the Mexican War in common. After their Mexican experience, both remained in the army—Lee climbing the ladder and Grant falling off the wagon and eventually out of the service.

Grant tried real estate and failed. He tried farming and failed. By the time of the Civil War he was relying on his father for a job as a tannery clerk.

Grant had tasted failure and did not fear it. He approached the battlefield much as he had approached personal matters, by squaring his shoulders and marching onward.

Grant's victories often started as encounters with failure, subjecting him to intense criticism, not only for the defeat but also for his continued, persistent pursuit of risky solutions.

Lincoln, however, found in Grant the quality his other generals often lacked.

"I can't spare this man," Lincoln told Grant's detractors. "He fights."

Into a Pickle and Out
FORT DONELSON, 1862

The gateway from the north into the western reaches of the Confederacy lay through Kentucky and Tennessee. Because of the sporadic nature of railroads in the area, three great rivers—the

Mississippi, Tennessee, and Cumberland—were the principal means of transport.

Confederate General Albert Sidney Johnston, commanding in the west, developed a strategy to control these pathways by establishing a string of outposts that not only placed artillery in command of the rivers but also provided a base from which troops could move overland as necessary.

On February 6, 1862, Federal troops under Grant's command accepted the surrender of the Rebel outpost at Fort Henry on the Tennessee River. The campaign had not been beautiful, but it had worked. Grant's troops had become bogged down in swampy terrain about eight miles upstream from the fort, but the Union's river navy had bombarded the fort into submission and the infantry arrived in time for the surrender.

Most of the Rebel troops in Fort Henry fled a few miles east to Fort Donelson on the Cumberland River. The new position, atop a 100-foot bluff, was further reinforced until it bristled with 20,000 men.

Grant's superior, General Henry Halleck, commander of the Western Theater, deemed Grant's position at Fort Henry to be risky and sent picks and shovels with orders to dig in against an anticipated Confederate counter-attack.

Never comfortable on the defensive, Grant telegraphed Halleck—six days after capturing Fort Henry—that he was taking his 15,000 men and advancing on Fort Donelson. Immediately after dispatching the message, Grant ordered the telegraph lines cut to prevent receipt of a counter-order.

Cocky from the ease of the Fort Henry exercise, Grant advanced without any plan other than to reprise what had worked before. He would surround the fort with infantry to prevent an escape and then bombard the living daylights out of it from navy gunboats.

This time the bombardment didn't work. The ships moved in too close and were pounded by shells from Confederate batteries

on the bluff above. Flag Officer Andrew Hull Foote, commanding the flotilla, urged Grant to give up the assault. Grant refused.

As he was riding back from the meeting with Foote, Grant
heard the sounds of battle. The Rebels were throwing 8,000 men
at the right end of the Union line to effect a breakout and open a
path to the south. The attack was succeeding; Union forces in the
area were in full retreat.

Rejecting the warnings of his commanders on the scene, Grant
ordered his troops to retake their previous positions. At the same
time, he ordered an attack on Fort Donelson from the side opposite the Rebel advance. That position was only lightly defended,
many Confederate soldiers having been moved to support the
breakout.

On the side of the breakout, Grant's counter-attack was working. The Rebel offensive slowed, aided by an amazing Rebel decision. Instead of strengthening their breakout position, the Rebel
troops were ordered to waste time gathering supplies for the
march south.

By nightfall, Grant's men had not only recovered from the
Rebel breakout assault but also were inside the last of the perim-
eter defenses on the fort's opposite side. The following morning
would find the new Union position reinforced with artillery to
rain shells on the Confederates sealed in Fort Donelson.

Considering himself too valuable to be caught, the fort's commander, Brigadier General John Floyd (who had been Secretary
of War in President Buchanan's cabinet) fled by boat that night.
Left in command was Brigadier General Simon Bolivar Bruckner,
a West Point classmate of Grant's. Their friendship was close
enough that Bruckner had loaned Grant money during one of his
difficult pre-war periods.

Before dawn Bruckner sent Grant a note asking for armistice
terms. Grant's reply, "No terms except unconditional and immediate surrender can be accepted. I propose to move immediately
upon your works."

Bruckner surrendered his entire army—17,000 men and sixty-five guns. It was a glorious victory for Grant, extracted from what had been an unwinnable situation only the day before. Counseled by his naval commander to give up and advised by his field subordinates that their line was irreparable, Grant had tenaciously soldiered on.

That tenacity not only brought victory but also a new nickname. Henceforth his men would say the initials "U.S." in their general's name stood not just for "Ulysses Simpson," but also for "Unconditional Surrender" Grant.

"I haven't despaired of whipping them yet"
THE BATTLE OF SHILOH, 1862

The fall of Fort Donelson opened the door to the western Confederacy for the Union. Grant—promoted to major general—now had 42,000 men in his Army of the Tennessee. In front of him, two icons commanded the Confederate troops—Albert Sidney Johnston and his number two, Pierre G. T. Beauregard. Johnston had commanded the U.S. Army's Western Department before the war. Beauregard was the hero of Fort Sumter and First Manassas (Bull Run).

With his forward line of forts lost, Johnston was determined to regroup the dispersed Confederate forces at Corinth, Mississippi, near the juncture of the Tennessee/Alabama/Mississippi borders. By the end of March 1862, Johnston had assembled 40,000 Rebels, ready to block any further Federal advance.

Grant had been ordered south to Pittsburg Landing, an old cotton-loading point on the Tennessee River, about twenty miles north of Corinth. He was awaiting the arrival of Major General Don Carlos Buell's Army of the Ohio. Together they would advance on the Confederates.

But the Rebels had another plan. They would attack Grant

before Buell arrived. On April 3, 1862, General Johnston's troops began the march north to Pittsburg Landing.

For General Grant, the Battle of Shiloh (named for a small church on the battlefield) was a management failure that beget a battlefield failure.

Despite known Rebel positions only twenty miles away, despite skirmishing among picket outposts, Grant's management failure allowed his men to be caught off guard. He had neither reconnoitered his front nor ordered his men to entrench.

"There will be no fighting here," he confidently—and erroneously—predicted to Buell in a message.

On the beautiful Sunday morning of April 6, all hell broke loose at Shiloh. The Rebels streamed out of the woods and caught the Bluecoats just beginning their morning routines. Grant was across the river having breakfast.

The Tennessee River in the rear, swampy Owl Creek on the right, and Lick Creek on the left bound the position of Grant's Union troops. As the Rebels poured in from the fourth side, the Union positions collapsed. If it hadn't been for about 2,000 men stubbornly standing their ground in the center of the line (dubbed the "Hornet's Nest" because of the ferocity of the zinging bullets), Grant's soldiers would have been smashed against the anvil of the river.

He may have been ill prepared, but in the face of adversity Grant was in his element. He sent word to Buell to hasten his march, called up gunboats on the river, order the siege guns intended to bombard Corinth spiked into place for use as field artillery, and rounded up the skedaddlers along the river. Grant seemed to be everywhere on the battlefield, placing units and directing artillery. His horse was killed under him, a bullet ripped his hat off, another went through his coat, and still another tore the insignia from his shoulder.

His tenacity was rewarded. Once again, Grant's opponent

committed the error of handing him an opportunity to snatch victory from sure defeat.

Instead of pushing around the Union resistance at the Hornet's Nest and taking it by envelopment, Johnston continued to hammer the position head-on. The Union line bent like a hairpin, but the center didn't break. What's more, in mid-afternoon, as Johnston was rallying his troops with the cry, "Once more and we have them," a Union bullet hit him in the leg, severing an artery. An hour later the Confederate leader had bled to death and General Beauregard was in command.

As night fell, the Rebels finally took the Hornet's Nest and Grant's lines were pushed deeper into the dead end formed by the river at his rear and the creeks on each flank.

"Well, Grant, we've had the devil's own day, haven't we?" lamented General William Tecumseh Sherman, who had been commanding the Union right.

"Yes," Grant replied. "Lick 'em tomorrow, though."

When General Buell arrived in the middle of the night with 25,000 new Federal troops, he was shocked by the catastrophe before him.

"What preparations have been made for retreating?" Buell inquired.

"I haven't despaired of whipping them yet," replied the tenacious Grant.

Brushing aside his previous failures, Grant was planning for victory. Aided by the fresh troops, the Union forces counterattacked in the morning and retook their old positions. Around mid-afternoon Beauregard ordered a Confederate retreat.

The Union forces, thanks to their general, were victorious. Other leaders might have lamented the day or, like General Buell advocated, retreated, but not Grant. As a result, Ulysses Grant turned defeat into victory in the greatest battle fought in North America up to that point.

Never Give Up!
VICKSBURG, 1862–63

Confederate President Jefferson Davis described the Mississippi River city of Vicksburg as "The nail that holds the halves of the Confederacy together."

At Fort Henry, Fort Donelson, and Shiloh, Ulysses S. Grant had eliminated Confederate positions on the Tennessee and Cumberland rivers. It now fell to him to pull the nail at Vicksburg.

Vicksburg, Mississippi, sits at a hairpin bend in the Big Muddy, across from Louisiana. By mid-1862, Union gunboats controlled the river north and south of the bend. By clinging to heavily fortified Vicksburg, however, the Rebels prevented the Federal fleets from uniting, thus maintaining a bridgehead to the western half of the Confederacy.

Vicksburg was called "the Gibraltar of the West"—and with good reason. The city was perched atop a 200-foot bluff. Its Confederate artillery batteries could command the river, while the Union boats couldn't elevate their guns high enough to return fire.

In June 1862, Federal naval units north and south of the city attempted to join their fleets and bombard "Gibraltar" with more than 200 cannon and twenty-three mortars. The Confederate guns on the top and sides of the escarpment were untouched.

Clearly, if Vicksburg was to be taken, it would not be from the Mississippi River. But the river wasn't Vicksburg's only natural defense. To the north, several thousand square miles of swamp protected it. The only dry approaches were from the east or south—through the heart of Confederate Mississippi and far from any Union base of operations.

Nevertheless, in late 1862, Grant set out from Memphis with 40,000 men of the Army of the Tennessee, heading south toward Vicksburg, 250 miles away, following the tracks of the Mississippi Central Railroad. The ever-lengthening Union supply line, however, was a ripe target for disruption by the Confederate cavalry. As he advanced, Grant was forced to leave troops along his route to protect his link with home.

At Grenada, Mississippi, 20,000 entrenched Confederates blocked Grant's depleted force. Meanwhile, behind the Union commander, Rebel cavalry raids tore up fifty miles of track, severed Grant's telegraph communications, and destroyed a Federal supply base.

Grant and his troops were stranded deep in enemy territory with retreat—failure—as the only option.

While Grant was trapped in enemy territory, his trusted lieutenant, William Tecumseh Sherman, was in a similar circumstance on another approach to Vicksburg.

Having advanced by transport barge down the Mississippi, Sherman attempted to penetrate the Yazoo swamp north of the city and catch the Rebels in a pincer with Grant's forces. The swamp, however, prevented Sherman from massing his troops against the Confederates, who were dug in on dry, high ground. Once again Grant's strategy ended in failure.

As the calendar changed to 1863, the Southerners clung fiercely to their "Gibraltar." The linchpin still held the two halves of the Confederacy together.

Unwilling to accept failure, Grant demonstrated his now famous tenacity once again.

If Vicksburg couldn't be captured, he reasoned, perhaps it could be circumvented. Grant concluded that by digging a canal through the open end of the hairpin, Union boat traffic on the Mississippi River could bypass Vicksburg altogether.

Grant issued his soldiers spades and set them to work digging a new river channel. Through January and February, they shoveled dirt instead of shouldering rifles. But the March rains quickly washed away their efforts, destroying the channel.

Once again, Grant had failed. Still, he persisted.

While some of his soldiers were fruitlessly trying to straighten out the hairpin turn, Grant had another corps farther upriver digging a six-mile canal which would connect the Mississippi with Lake Providence, once part of the river but now isolated and landlocked. From there, he could connect with smaller rivers flowing south, thereby opening a waterway around Vicksburg for Union boats.

But the first boat through this bypass tore its bottom out on a forest of submerged stumps. Once again, Grant's efforts ended in failure.

With the spring came new efforts by Grant to take Vicksburg by force of arms. Again, Vicksburg's geography prevailed. Two efforts were launched simultaneously using the Union navy to ferry troops through the Yazoo swamps north of the city. The attempts came to naught. The roots and branches of the cypress and cottonwood trees tore at the boat bottoms and broke off anything above deck. The Confederates used logs to block the narrow channels through the swamp. In one instance, at Steele's Bayou, Sherman had to march his men from transport barges several miles through the swamp mud to rescue a Federal navy flotilla, which was in danger of being captured.

Two more months had been wasted. Two more failures for Grant.

Grant had tried everything, including, literally, changing the face of the earth. The result was clear-cut failure . . . again, and again, and again, and again, and again, and again. Six times in all.

Politicians, the public, and the press were losing confidence and patience.

"This campaign is badly managed," wrote one of Grant's subordinate generals to his brother in Congress. "I fear a calamity before Vicksburg . . . all Grant's schemes have failed."

Rumors that Grant was drinking heavily spread. The congressional delegation from his home state of Illinois warned Lincoln that leaving Grant in command of troops from that state imperiled Republican electoral chances.

Under the guise of investigating paymaster accounts, Lincoln dispatched Assistant Secretary of War Charles Dana to scrutinize Grant.

Nevertheless, Grant refused to admit defeat. At this low point in his career, Grant's tenacity kept him focused on his objective. Well aware of the intrigue against him, Grant began to plan and implement an innovative strategy to capture Vicksburg that flew in the face of military wisdom. Even the loyal Sherman questioned Grant's plan.

Undaunted by his six previous failures, Ulysses S. Grant proceeded to rewrite the textbook of military tactics. To do so, he drew on a lesson he had learned in one of his early Vicksburg failures. In his first attack on Vicksburg, Grant had found himself cut off from his supply lines as a result of the activities of the Confederate cavalry. But being cut off from his supplies had led to a discovery. "I was amazed at the quantity of supplies the country afforded," he observed in his *Memoirs*. "This taught me a lesson."

The lesson was that his troops could live off the land. Grant decided to maneuver against Vicksburg from the south, advancing through enemy territory while completely cut off from his base, without supply lines for food or forage. The commander marched his Union troops down the west bank of the Mississippi, opposite Vicksburg, out of range of Confederate guns, to a point about thirty miles below the city.

To cross the mile-wide Mississippi, however, required the transports and barges of the Union navy from above Vicksburg. For two nights, the fleet ran the Rebel gauntlet, losing a few ships and barges, but arriving with sufficient capacity to ferry Grant's army across the river. On April 30, 1863, the Union troops successfully crossed the Mississippi. Instead of marching north to attack Vicksburg, however, Grant marched east, deeper into the Confederacy, defeating the Rebel force at Jackson, Mississippi. Having thus secured his rear, Grant moved upon Vicksburg.

In the first seventeen days after landing on Confederate soil, Grant's troops marched 180 miles. They won five battles, and drove the Rebel defenders into fortified Vicksburg—all the while living off the land.

While the Confederates dug in and opposed Grant's advance, the geography that had repeatedly thwarted the Union general now became his ally. Because of Grant's tenacity, the Union now controlled the flat, dry, usable southern and eastern approaches by which the city was supplied. Laying siege, Grant determined to starve out the Rebels.

Six weeks later, on July 4, 1863 (coincidentally, a day after the Confederates lost the Battle of Gettysburg in the east), the "Gibraltar of the West" surrendered. Grant succeeded with his seventh attempt to capture Vicksburg.

With the fall of Vicksburg, the Confederacy was split in two. What's more, Union forces now had what Grant had previously lacked—a supply line into the underbelly of the Rebel states.

"When you first reached the vicinity of Vicksburg," Lincoln wrote Grant, "I never had any faith, except a general hope, that the Yazoo Pass expedition and the like [i.e., the early failures] could succeed—when you got below . . . I thought you should go down the river and join Gen. Banks [at Baton Rouge]; and when you turned northward east of the Big Black river, I feared it was a mistake—I now wish to make the personal acknowledgment that you were right, and I was wrong."

Ulysses S. Grant, vilified only weeks before, was suddenly a national hero on the strength of his personal purpose and tenacity. Shortly thereafter, as a result of Grant's stunning victory, he was given command of the Union armies in the west.

From Defense to Offense
CHATTANOOGA, 1863

About ten weeks after the fall of Vicksburg, the Union army in Tennessee, commanded by Major General William S. Rosecrans, was defeated at the Battle of Chickamauga. The survivors fled to nearby Chattanooga.

On the banks of the Tennessee River, Chattanooga took its name from an Indian word meaning "mountains looking at each other." The Confederates held those mountains and used their positions to stop Chattanooga from receiving supplies either by river or by the main road from the west. The only open supply route into town was from the north, along winding mountain trails that would soon be closed by winter.

Confederate President Jefferson Davis, looking down on the city from the Rebel position gloated, "Before another week that army is my own!" The peripatetic Union Assistant Secretary of War Charles Dana came to the same conclusion. With 11,000 horses and mules dead and no way to transport artillery, ammunition, or supplies to the isolated Union force, surrender seemed imminent.

Since Grant had been given command in the west, the matter was now his problem. As a first step, he fired General Rosecrans, the man responsible for the mess, and wired the new commander, Major General George Thomas, "Hold Chattanooga at all hazards. I will be there as soon as possible."

Thomas' reply was just what Grant wanted to hear: "I will hold the town until we starve."

Union Major General Joseph Hooker was ordered from Virginia with 20,000 troops and Sherman's men from the Army of the Tennessee marched from Vicksburg. If the 35,000 men in Chattanooga could hold out until their arrival, Grant would have a powerful offensive punch.

But first, the siege had to be broken. Ulysses S. Grant rode into town on October 23. Five days later he wired Washington, "I think the question of supplies must now be regarded as settled . . . preparations may commence for offensive operations."

A plan for breaking the siege had been developed by Rosecrans' staff, but "Old Rosey" never put it into effect. Grant knew no such reservations. On his first full day in town Grant went to check out the feasibility of the plan by familiarizing himself with the geography of Chattanooga. What Grant found was a city on the south bank of a lazily meandering river. Immediately west of town the river took a sharp turn south, then a hairpin turn north, wandered through some mountains, and turned south again. To bring supplies in from the west—the only feasible route since the south and east were Rebel territory and the mountain trails from the north were about to be made impassable by winter—it was necessary to cross the river three times. And the Rebels controlled all but the one crossing directly behind the town.

Grant ordered Hooker to march to the westernmost crossing by night and to hide until the plan was hatched. Thomas sent one detachment out from Chattanooga toward the second crossing. The masterstroke came, however, when 1,300 Federal troops floated silently down the Tennessee under cover of night, using bridge pontoons for their transport. After a six-mile float, the waterborne troops surprised the Rebel detachment guarding the crossing and the pontoons were used to build a bridge across the river.

With Hooker's and Thomas' men now guarding the two key river crossings, the supply line to Chattanooga was open again. The men, back at full rations, dubbed it the "Cracker Line."

Less than a month later, resupplied and with Sherman's troops in camp, Grant went on the offensive. The first day, Thomas took the Rebel picket outposts in the center of the Confederate line. The second day, Hooker took Lookout Mountain on the Confederate left end while Sherman became bogged down assaulting the right. The third day's plan was for Hooker and Sherman to march toward each other, rolling up the Rebel position atop Missionary Ridge.

That plan didn't work. Hooker stopped to rebuild a destroyed bridge thwarting his advance and Sherman remained bottled up by a steep-walled ravine the map said didn't exist. (When Sherman sent word back to Grant of his predicament, he received a simple reply, "Attack again.")

Thomas' advance against the center of the Confederate line on Missionary Ridge was the day's biggest surprise. The troops were just supposed to be applying pressure to help those on the wings.

Upon taking the Rebels' first defensive line, however, Thomas' men found their position untenable because of fire from above. On their own volition, starting first in small groups and then in unison, they surged up the mountain. Grant, observing this, turned to Thomas and asked, "Who ordered those men up the ridge?" Thomas, just as stunned, replied, "I don't know. I did not."

The Confederates fled—for thirty miles.

Grant had prevailed again by simply refusing to accept what he found. He fired the commander who created the mess; solved the supply problem with a bold stroke; and when things didn't go as planned on the field, kept pushing forward until a solution presented itself.

The bankrupt tannery clerk was the talk of the nation. Shortly thereafter Ulysses S. Grant was given command of all U.S. armies, becoming the first man since George Washington to hold the rank of lieutenant general.

Lee Discovers the Grant Tenacity
VIRGINIA, 1864

Upon assuming supreme command, Grant made Robert E. Lee's Army of Northern Virginia his special target.

Six generals had commanded Union forces in the east by the

time Grant rode into camp. All had been humiliated by Confederate troops. If the Rebels were to be stopped, it had to begin by defeating Lee.

Since the beginning of the war, the script for Lee's soldiers had almost always been the same—hand the Bluecoats a licking, watch them crawl away, then maneuver to do it all over again. Thus, while Grant may have been in charge of all Union armies everywhere, he determined to make his headquarters with the Army of the Potomac and to personally do battle with Robert E. Lee.

In March 1864, Grant arrived at the winter quarters of the Army of the Potomac in Virginia, situated across the Rapidan River from where the Confederates were wintering. By the first week in May, the new Union commander had his army on the move.

Grant's plan was to cross the Rapidan and move around Lee's right flank toward Richmond—drawing the Rebels out of their fortifications and forcing them into a pitched battle in open fields where the Union's superiority in men and matériel could deliver a knockout blow. Grant's forces outnumbered Lee's nearly two to one.

To accomplish his plan, Grant first had to maneuver his force through the Wilderness, a junglelike thicket of second-growth trees, vines, and scrub brush which Lee had used so effectively only a year before in his greatest victory, at Chancellorsville (see Lesson Four).

Grant planned for the Army of the Potomac to march through the Wilderness in forty-eight hours, before Lee could mobilize to stop him. To be confronted in that thick forest by the Rebels would neutralize the Union's advantages in artillery and manpower.

But Grant's new command was not noted for its speed. And on May 5, Grant's second day on the move, Lee's forces caught the Union army still slogging through the Wilderness.

For two days some of the most horrific combat of the war raged, amid the unburied skeletons of soldiers killed a year earlier in the Battle of Chancellorsville. Troops trained in formation combat were forced to break into small units for what was described as "bushwhacking on a grand scale." Visibility was so poor in the gloom of the dense growth that veterans reported "firing by ear."

Brush fires, ignited by the sparks from weapons and fanned by evening breezes, further obscured visibility and burned the undergrowth and the wounded indiscriminately. The fires set off gunpowder in cartridge boxes on the waists of the injured, who mercifully died from their own exploding bullets rather than being roasted alive.

In two days, Grant sustained 17,500 casualties, at least 7,000 more than his opponent and even more than in General Hooker's Chancellorsville fiasco in the same area a year earlier.

"Lee had never beaten an adversary so soundly as he had beaten this one in the course of . . . two days," commented Shelby Foote in his classic history, *The Civil War*.

Thus, when the Union supply wagons began pulling out, the veterans in the Union ranks assumed that history was repeating itself. Yet another commander had led them to defeat and was now retreating to lick his wounds.

However, this time the wagons were pulling out to support a Union *advance*.

Coming to a crossroads in the smoldering forest, where one road led north and the other deeper into Virginia, the tenacious Grant turned south. His battered and battle-weary troops cheered and followed their general, surely a different kind of commander than they were accustomed to. For the first time in the war, the Army of the Potomac, having failed to achieve a victory, was advancing instead of retreating.

"Whatever happens, there will be no turning back," Grant messaged Lincoln in the aftermath of the Wilderness battle. The message so delighted the President that he embraced the messenger, a newspaper reporter, and kissed him on his forehead.

The Federal commander took the offensive once again, marching southeastward, a maneuver designed to skirt the right flank of the Rebel force and place Union troops in the vicinity of Spotsylvania Court House, between Lee and the Confederate capital at Richmond. Knowing that Lee must defend Richmond at all costs, Grant planned to dig in and force the Confederate commander to attack him.

Lee, however, anticipated Grant's maneuver and began preparing for a race to get to Spotsylvania first. Since Grant was in position to march on the most direct roads, Lee put his infantry to work hacking a shortcut through the woods. In addition, he sent his swift cavalry units ahead to build fortifications at Spotsylvania.

The Confederate infantry won the race, but barely, arriving just before Grant's Bluecoats. Lee's troops took possession of a fence-rail breastworks built by the cavalry troopers, an ideal defensive position.

For the next ten days, the Confederates strengthened that position, dubbed the Mule Shoe because of its semicircular shape. They resisted one Union attack after another. Spotsylvania became synonymous with brutal assaults and equally brutal repulses, including, on May 12, eighteen solid hours of often hand-to-hand fighting at the apex of the curved fortifications. The troops appropriately named the apex "the Bloody Angle."

Again, Lee had stymied Grant.

But the tenacious general who had persisted to victory after six defeats at Vicksburg was not about to give up. In the midst of the fighting at Spotsylvania, he sent another message of resolve to Lincoln, "I propose to fight it out on this line if it takes all summer."

Fulfilling that commitment, Grant moved left around Spotsylvania and plunged further southward, this time racing Lee twenty-five miles to a rail junction across the North Anna River. Again, the Rebel commander got there first, with ample time to dig in before his rival arrived. Grant tried only a couple of probing actions before again jogging left around Lee's flank and continuing his march toward Richmond.

Moving twenty miles further south, Grant found that Lee had, yet again, arrived first and entrenched his Rebel troops behind Totopotomy Creek. For two more days, the Union troops probed the Confederate positions before once more sliding around Lee's right flank and heading southward. By now, Grant was only nine miles northeast of Richmond.

The bloody month of May 1864 ended with Grant's cavalry racing ahead to seize the next objective before Lee could get there. On May 31 and June 1, Union horsemen bested their Southern counterparts to capture the crossroads of Cold Harbor. Both sides dug in for a decisive battle.

On June 3, Grant ordered a head-on assault against the Confederate position. In sixty minutes, 7,000 men were killed or wounded.

"I regret this assault more than any one I have ever ordered," Grant mourned later that day.

In Grant's first month of campaigning with the Army of the Potomac, he had incurred a staggering 44,000 casualties. And he didn't have a single overall battlefield victory to show for it.

With incomprehensible amounts of blood on his hands, the eyes of the entire world upon him, and the criticism of political enemies again assailing him, U. S. Grant remained true to his credo. He attacked.

By repeatedly maneuvering around Lee's right flank, Grant had led his battered army to the doorstep of the Confederate capital. Now he would try the tactic one more time, but with the variation of applying pressure on the Rebel forces at three points simultaneously.

To his troops in the Shenandoah Valley, Grant issued orders to cross the Blue Ridge Mountains and head toward Richmond, smashing everything in their way. He sent two divisions of his cavalry to form a pincer with the approaching Shenandoah Valley units.

And for the main force of his army, Grant planned to fall upon the enemy's rear, in a replay of Vicksburg, by seizing the key rail junction at Petersburg, just south of Richmond. Grant knew Lee could not defend Richmond if this supply line were cut. A Federal force south of Richmond, blocking Lee's supplies, would also make it less likely that the Rebels could spare the men or matériel to threaten Washington.

In a flurry of activity designed to confuse Lee about his true intentions, Grant disengaged from Cold Harbor and swiftly marched to the James River.

At Petersburg on the James, the Union troops found a physical monument to the boldness of their leader's vision—the longest pontoon bridge ever built. Grant had ordered his engineers to build a bridge 2,100 feet long and sturdy enough to withstand the strong currents of the James as well as the river's four-foot tidal rise and fall.

On June 14, Grant's troops began doing the impossible— crossing the James at one of its widest points, with Richmond in their sights.

Unfortunately, once on the other side of the river, Grant's hesitant corps commanders failed to display as much initiative as their leader. After a mad scramble, Lee arrived with most of his troops in time to blunt the Union advance.

Nevertheless, Grant, in only six weeks, had marched the Union army eighty miles overland, nearly to the outskirts of Richmond, against the finest military mind the Confederacy could field and against an army which had regularly routed Grant's predecessors.

Because Grant's tenacity would not allow him to accept the defeats repeatedly handed to him along the way, his Federal forces had fought their way to a position just south of the Confederate capital. There, well supplied by water transport, Grant and his men settled into a siege.

Nine months later Richmond fell and within weeks Robert E. Lee had surrendered.

Tenacity at the Dawn of the Electronic Age
HOME BOX OFFICE

In overcoming repeated setbacks to make the Home Box Office premium cable channel a success, ex-divinity student-turned-lawyer-turned-cable-executive Jerry Levin needed to draw on the same tenacity and persistence that had made Ulysses S. Grant so successful.

He demonstrated the raw tenacity required by any insurgent with a new idea in the face of overwhelming opposition by the incumbents.

Chuck Dolan, a pioneering cable TV visionary, had conceived HBO—originally named the Green Channel—as an add-on subscription service offering movies and sports to provide desperately needed revenue for his New York City cable system. To increase revenue from the service still more, he decided to transmit HBO via a chain of microwave towers to cable systems in other areas. In early November 1972, HBO began transmitting movies to 325 customers in Wilkes-Barre, Pennsylvania. One hundred days after its launch, Time Inc., which was financing Dolan, put in thirty-three-year-old Jerry Levin to run things.

The operation Levin headed was little more than an experiment without a very bright future. In order to build HBO into a success, Levin would have to battle an army of powerful adversaries: broadcast television networks, theater owners, major league sports teams, unimaginative cable system operators, the Federal Communications Commission, and even his own employer, Time Inc.

Among the media icons of the twentieth century were the magazines of Time Inc.—*Time*, *Life*, *Fortune*, and *Sports Illustrated*. The corporate descendants of Time's founder, Henry Luce, were publishers, men so devoted to ink-on-paper that they sold off the radio and television stations they owned across the country. Having effectively foreclosed on Chuck Dolan to take ownership of his New York City cable system, the print-oriented Time Inc. decided it didn't want its new asset. Manhattan Cable and its struggling premium channel, Home Box Office, went on the block. Warner Communications agreed to buy the properties. The City of New York, however, refused to approve transfer of the franchise.

Guttenberg's descendants who ran Time Inc. were thus stuck with electronic properties they neither wanted nor understood. Jerry Levin got to hold the HBO tar baby.

Levin's unwanted corporate stepchild was trying to succeed where much mightier names had previously failed. The first attempt at pay TV—led by television legend Pat Weaver, creator of "Today" and "The Tonight Show"—came a cropper when California movie theater operators scared the state's voters into passing a referendum prohibiting subscription television.

Thus, while trying to develop a business model, Levin also had to contend with broadcasters and theater owners who were warning of "The End of Free TV" in order to smother the new competitor. Their efforts were successful. At the behest of the anti-HBO forces, the Federal Communications Commission (FCC) adopted a blatantly restrictive regulation prohibiting cable systems from showing movies that were between two and ten years old.

Movies more than ten years old were hardly the fare likely to stimulate viewer demand. And movies less than two years old were still playing theaters in the small towns, so Hollywood had no desire to jeopardize that revenue by licensing the films to HBO.

Broadcasters and theater owners were not the only businesses trying to stifle the upstart premium channel. Major league sports teams had negotiated lucrative local TV contracts based upon artificial scarcity created by limiting the number of games that could be broadcast. HBO wanted to open new markets for more games, but the team owners wanted nothing to do with changing the profitable status quo and froze out HBO.

Like Grant's opponents on the Mississippi, the companies threatened by HBO occupied the economic heights and were entrenched in fortified positions.

And, like Grant, Levin responded to these obstacles by attacking. He sued the FCC to overturn the pay cable rules. Likewise, he dared the sports team owners to come after him for rebroadcasting games into markets where they weren't being shown.

Despite Levin's aggressive response, however, the paucity of programming had a negative effect on his struggling channel. By late 1973, at the end of its first year of operations, HBO's subscribership had fallen to 8,323 from a high of 12,500. More subscribers were leaving HBO each month than were signing up.

This subscriber churn problem was exacerbated by the fact that cable system operators—upon whom HBO relied to sell the service to customers—were terrible marketers. A hearty band of entrepreneurs, cable system operators were engineering-oriented. Their focus was on building and maintaining an electronic distribution system, not on marketing programs.

As 1974 began, Jerry Levin decided he couldn't rely on the cable system operators to determine HBO's future. So, he put his own sales team to work, and it paid off almost immediately. For the first time in almost a year, HBO began signing up more subscribers than it lost.

By the spring of 1974, HBO had climbed to 15,000 subscribers, 2,500 above 1973's high point. Despite the growth in viewers, however, Time's president, Jim Shepley, delivered an ultimatum to Levin—20,000 subscribers by June or face a shut-down.

Sounding like a general, Levin told his subordinates in a memo, "As of June 30: the magic number is 20,000. There are no ands, ifs or buts about it."

The goal was met, thanks to a little fudging which "lost" the paperwork for a few hundred disconnect orders.

HBO was still alive—but barely. Tenacity had gotten Levin to this point. Now it was time to take a Grant-like bold risk.

In late 1973, Levin had seen the future in a parking lot in the shadow of Disney's Tomorrowland in Anaheim, California. The organizers of the annual National Cable Television Association convention had erected a huge satellite earth station in the lot to receive a television signal originating in Washington, D.C., by which Speaker of the House Carl Albert addressed the assemblage.

That pioneering satellite transmission gave Levin an idea. Using point-to-multi-point satellite transmission, he could reliably deliver HBO's programming to thousands of cable systems simultaneously instead of depending on a chain of risky and more expensive point-to-point microwave links. In the satellite, Levin saw the capability to expand his reach and cut his distribution costs at the same time. "To sustain Time Inc.'s interest, we needed a big idea," Levin later told *Cable World* magazine.

And talk about risk! In 1974, when Jerry Levin signed a six-year, $1.25 million annual contract to send his HBO signal to cable systems by geostationary satellite, the channel's monthly revenue was only about $300,000. In other words, Levin committed himself to pay an amount equal to almost five months of each year's total revenue just for satellite distribution!

As if that financial risk weren't great enough, the FCC insisted that the satellite dishes needed to receive the signal had to be twenty-five feet in diameter—a $100,000 investment for a cable system operator to try an as-yet unproven premium channel. Furthermore, the FCC required that HBO apply for agency permission to transmit its signal—at the very time HBO was suing the FCC!

For almost three years Jerry Levin had battled to keep HBO alive against opposition from every conceivable corner.

Like Grant, whenever something went against him, Jerry Levin just kept attacking. And now Jerry Levin was going to bet the farm on another attack, the untried concept of relaying television programs from a satellite 22,300 miles out in space.

It was a bold vision worthy of Grant's brilliant rewriting of military tactics at Vicksburg or the general's daring construction of history's longest pontoon bridge at Petersburg.

Levin's tenacious boldness caught his opponents unprepared. The idea of bouncing a television network off a satellite was so preposterous that the broadcasters, Hollywood, and sports leagues didn't even challenge HBO's request for permission at the FCC.

Levin launched HBO's satellite service in September 1975, with a bang. Using multiple satellites, he brought the Muhammad Ali–Joe Frazier "Thrilla in Manila" heavyweight championship fight *live* into American living rooms. Instead of waiting hours for videotape to be flown to an originating point, Americans were able to see a live event from half a world away.

Today, we take for granted that satellites deliver live television instantly to every place on earth. But in 1975, live video from a satellite was something found only in Arthur C. Clarke's science fiction—and Jerry Levin's vision.

Immediately after the "Thrilla in Manila," the average of new HBO subscribers soared to 30,000 a month.

In March 1977, the U.S. Court of Appeals, in the *HBO* decision, finally struck down the FCC's rules protecting broadcasters and theater owners, essentially deregulating pay cable.

By the end of 1978, Levin's refusal to buckle in the face of numerous obstacles had made Home Box Office a success. Levin had transformed Time Inc. from a publishing company into an electronic media company, with 46 percent of its profits coming from the video division and only 36 percent from publishing.

In 1990, Jerry Levin, now a top executive of the parent company, engineered the merger of Time Inc. and Warner Communications to become the world's largest media empire.

As Lincoln had promoted Grant for his leadership, so was Levin promoted for his. In 1992, Jerry Levin was named Chief Executive of Time Warner.

Marching Orders

"It took fifteen years to become an overnight success," I once heard a Tony Award winner comment wryly in accepting the award. Success rarely comes without persistence and tenacity.

It's impossible for a leader to avoid problems, mishaps, or failures. Such are the consequences of making decisions.

Successful leaders make a choice not to accept the setbacks. In the process, they open up the potential for success.

Because U. S. Grant and Jerry Levin tenaciously hung in, they were still in the battle, available to take advantage of new developments, including the mistakes of their opponents.

Failure to tenaciously hang on means you aren't around when opportunity presents itself.

Leaders press on, with persistence, until they win.

Lesson Three

Yesterday's Tactics Make Today's Defeats

Embrace change

The battlefield, whether corporate or military, produces a Darwinian imperative—evolve or face defeat and extinction. Victory belongs to those who innovate.

Civil War leaders, schooled on the tactics of Napoleon, saw those tactics die a bloody death at the hands of new technology. Confederate General Robert E. Lee was brilliantly audacious and combative, but surprisingly closed-minded when circumstances changed. Union Major General Philip Sheridan, on the other hand, became Ulysses S. Grant's implement of change in the war's final months, re-writing tactics and eventually defeating Lee's army.

Today's leaders confront change at a faster pace than their Civil War counterparts, making it necessary to be even more receptive to change and agile in response. Continuing to fight the next battle the same way as the last one is as much an invitation to defeat in the executive suite as it is in war.

Leaders who fail to recognize and embrace innovation lose their battles as surely as those who adapt overwhelm their competition.

Adieu Napoleon

The pre–Civil War United States Army was obsessed with Napoleon. West Point—the training ground for the generals of both North and South—was a model of the French military academy where all cadets were required to learn French in order to read Bonaparte in his mother tongue. Even the standard army manual, *Rifle and Light Infantry Tactics,* was almost a direct translation of the similar French manual. Napoleonic thinking permeated both the Confederate and Union tactical doctrine.

The problem was Napoleon's last battle had been fought almost fifty years in the past. A lot can change in fifty years.

Bonaparte's army was a blunt instrument using imprecise, short-range weapons. Masses of men would advance until they finally could fight hand-to-hand. Massed cavalry would charge, swinging sabers, to try to break the enemy's line. And artillery was massed to blow a hole in the enemy's position.

Napoleon's success lay in the fact that while his opponents kept fighting according to even older tactics, he evolved a more mobile and devastating style of warfare. It was precisely because of his innovations that Napoleon was studied at West Point. However, by slavishly following doctrines that had worked for Napoleon a half century earlier, his American acolytes forgot the master's greatest lesson—the imperative of innovation.

Lee Fails to Adapt
GETTYSBURG, DAY THREE, 1863

Confederate General Robert E. Lee was the Napoleon of the Civil War. Bonaparte's great innovations—holding the enemy's front while maneuvering into his rear or falling upon a divided enemy from a central position—were the paint on Lee's palette.

During his first year in command this worked so well that the Army of Northern Virginia seemed almost invincible. The Rebel troops began to believe their general—Marse Robert, they called him in their drawl—could do no wrong. They would follow him anywhere.

The trouble was that while Napoleon's strategic maneuvers were timeless classics, technology had changed their tactical implementation. Lee's tactics were leading his men back to the turn of the century battlefields of Europe. Fighting battles in the sixth decade of the nineteenth century by following Napoleon's blunt application of mass, as Lee would discover, had become obsolete, even suicidal.

After a year of being "on a roll," Lee led the Army of Northern Virginia north again. It was time to give Virginia a respite from the fighting. It was time to give the Northerners a taste of warfare on *their* territory. Hopefully, a few victories on Northern soil would convince Abraham Lincoln to accept a negotiated settlement for an independent Confederacy.

The Pennsylvania farm town of Gettysburg became the highwater mark of the Confederate army. After two days of fighting, the Rebels had pushed the Federals through the town and had hit hard on both flanks. Now, on the third day, General Lee concluded, a strike at the center of the Union position would be decisive.

General Lee sent 15,000 men, under Major General George Pickett, marching in tight-packed Napoleonic ranks with parade ground precision across three quarters of a mile of open field to assault the Union forces dug in atop Cemetery Ridge.

As Civil War historian Bruce Catton described the charge in *Glory Road*:

"There it was, for the last time in this war, and perhaps for the last time anywhere, the grand pageantry and color of war in the old style . . . fighting men lined up for a mile and a half from flank to flank . . . soldiers marching forward elbow to elbow . . . lines dressed as if for a parade . . ."

Such head-on assaults had enabled Napoleon to conquer Europe. Lee had personally seen them work in Mexico. This time, however, the tactic failed disastrously. Over 7,000 Confederate troops were slaughtered, principally because of a new technology—the addition of little grooves to the inside of a musket's barrel, grooves that didn't exist at the time of Napoleon or the Mexican War.

Lee had the grace to accept personal responsibility for persisting in disastrously outmoded tactics.

"It's my fault," Lee declared to the survivors straggling back to the Confederate lines. "It is I who have lost this fight."

And indeed, it was.

Lee had stubbornly refused to adjust his battlefield tactics in response to changes in military weaponry.

Napoleonic doctrine dictated a march of a mass of men to within 50 to 100 yards of their objective, where the troops would stop and deliver volleys of bullets into the opposing army. The soldiers of those times didn't even sight their weapons, so poor was their accuracy. But enough men firing enough bullets could make up in volume what they lacked in precision.

Of course, until the Civil War, the enemy was equipped with equally inaccurate weapons, so engagements usually ended up being decided when one side collapsed or when the two sides were close enough to go after each other with bayonets and sabers.

The infantry weapon of Napoleon's time was the flintlock smoothbore musket. When Lee fought in Mexico, thirty years after Napoleon's last battle, troops still used smoothbores and the principal technical change had only been the replacement of the flintlock firing mechanism with the percussion cap.

In a smoothbore musket, the ignited gunpowder unevenly pushed a heavy round musket ball down the gun barrel. Once out of the muzzle, the musket ball behaved aerodynamically much like a baseball pitcher's erratic curve ball.

"At a distance of a few hundred yards, a man might fire at you all day without your finding it out," Ulysses S. Grant wrote in his *Memoirs,* describing his Mexican War experience against the inaccurate smoothbore muskets.

The year after the Mexican War ended, a French army officer, Claude Étienne Minié, developed a method for increasing the range and accuracy of muskets. Unfortunately for the men of Pickett's Charge, they and their Civil War comrades were among the guinea pigs on whom the new technology was tested.

It had been known for years that rifling the barrel of a gun—putting spiral grooves on the walls inside the barrel—increased the accuracy of the projectile by giving it spin. However, the grooves became clogged with gunpowder residue that had to be cleaned every few rounds—not a practical idea in the middle of a battle.

Minié, however, developed a cylindrical bullet with a concave base (not unlike the indentation in the bottom of a bottle of French champagne). The indentation trapped the exploding gas and expanded the bullet to fit tightly against the walls of the barrel, cleaning out the gunpowder residue from the previous shot as it passed down the barrel.

Minié's mechanics were impeccable. His results were deadly. Not only was the bullet more accurate as a result of the spin imparted by the rifling but also gas trapped behind the bullet, as opposed to escaping around a ball, increased its range.

Whereas a smoothbore weapon had a maximum range of 400 to 500 yards and an accurate range of only about 100 yards, a rifle bullet could travel over 1,000 yards and could accurately hit a target as far away as 500 yards.

Ironically, it was Secretary of War Jefferson Davis—later President of the Confederacy—who, in 1855, ordered the U.S. Army to begin converting from the smoothbore to the rifled musket. When Lee faced the Union army at Gettysburg, over 70 percent of the Federal troops were equipped with rifles. A smaller, but not insignificant, percentage of Lee's troops also had rifles.

No longer was it necessary to march troops to within a few yards of each other to inflict damage. Fighting could be conducted at longer range, thus favoring a dug-in defense that could pick off an assaulting force as it advanced. Troops advancing in parade ground order, as Napoleonic theory decreed, became as vulnerable as shooting gallery targets.

At Pickett's Charge, the route of the attack made the situation even worse. Lee ordered the 15,000 Confederate soldiers to march in tight-packed formation on an angled path which took them in front of approximately 40,000 Union soldiers, most of them with accurate rifles.

When Pickett gave his command—"Up men and to your posts! Don't forget today that you are from old Virginia!"—he was approximately 1,400 yards from the Union line. This meant that after the first 400 yards, his men were within range of the Union rifles. The men then had to proceed more than a half mile under fire, while still marching as if in a parade. As a result, only 150 rebels actually made it to their intended objective.

It didn't have to end so tragically. Even before Lee and his Army of Northern Virginia crossed the Potomac River into Union territory and headed toward Pennsylvania, his most trusted lieutenant, General James L. Longstreet, tried to convince the Confederate commander to change.

Longstreet argued that the old tactic of marching ranks of tightly packed soldiers against an entrenched enemy was outdated and potentially catastrophic when the enemy was armed with the accurate rifled muskets. He urged Lee to adopt a new "tactical defensive" maneuver, establishing Confederate troops in strategically important positions, and waiting to pick off the Union forces when they attacked. That tactic had worked successfully for the Confederacy only seven months earlier at the Battle of Fredericksburg.

But at Gettysburg, Lee rejected the advice.

Longstreet was adapting to the new reality of the battlefield. Lee was not.

"The 15,000 men who could make a successful assault over that field has never been arrayed for battle," Longstreet told Lee.

"The enemy is up there," Lee replied, referring to the Union troops dug in on Cemetery Ridge, "and I am going to attack him there."

"I do not want to make this charge," Longstreet told a subordinate a moment before Pickett's doomed soldiers stepped off. "I do not see how it can succeed."

Unfortunately for Lee and the 15,000 Confederates involved in the charge, Longstreet was right.

Lessons Lost and Lessons Learned
THE CAVALRY

At the outset of the war, both the Confederate and Union armies had high expectations for the cavalry. During the Mexican War there had been numerous grand and glorious cavalry charges. The horsemen produced on the plains of Mexico the same success they had on the fields of Europe, shattering infantry formations with a pell-mell rush of horseflesh and steel.

But gun barrel grooves changed that.

In Napoleon's cavalry, charging horsemen needed only survive the first volley of musket fire in order to fall upon the infantry before it could reload. The Union army manual *Cavalry Tactics* codified this procedure. In a charge against infantry, the cavalry troopers were to trot to within 200 paces of the enemy, then proceed forward at an increasing rate, reaching a full gallop fifty to sixty paces from the enemy line. The thundering hooves and slashing sabers would wreak havoc on the infantry's formation. The tactic worked splendidly until Minié's innovation increased the effective range of a rifle so that the troopers could come under accurate fire hundreds of yards before they even formed for the assault.

For the most part, the cavalry of both the North and South evolved to reflect this new reality. Instead of dashing charges, the horsemen's role was recast into less glamorous activities such as reconnaissance, pursuit of a defeated enemy, covering the retreats as well as the flanks of infantry, screening infantry movements, and rounding up the shirkers and skedaddlers.

But this new reality galled those who had joined the cavalry for its offensive glamour and the promotion and fame they expected to follow. One of those was a brigadier general of the Union cavalry—Hugh Judson Kilpatrick.

General Kilpatrick, valedictorian of the last West Point class before the war, intended to parlay battlefield fame into political office, possibly including the presidency. Immediately following Pickett's Charge, Kilpatrick made the identical mistake Lee did, using tactics from a previous war.

After the withdrawal of Pickett's men, Kilpatrick ordered a cavalry charge against the far right of the Confederate line. The officer ordered to lead the charge, Brigadier General Elon J. Farnsworth, in an echo of Longstreet's warning to Lee, counseled against the maneuver. The Rebels had superior numbers, a good position in which cavalry would be hampered by woods and the boulder-strewn ground—and the Confederates had rifles.

Kilpatrick ordered the charge anyway.

"General, do you mean it?" Farnsworth asked when given the order. "[T]hese are too good men to kill!"

"Do you refuse to obey my orders?" Kilpatrick flared. "If you are afraid to lead this charge, I will lead it."

Standing in his stirrups, Farnsworth defended his honor against the imputation of cowardice. Kilpatrick backed off, but refused to rescind the order.

The last words Farnsworth spoke to his leader were, "General, if you order the charge, I will lead it, but you must take the responsibility." The 1st Vermont Cavalry proceeded to demonstrate how the rifle had eliminated the effectiveness of the Napoleonic cavalry charge.

Kilpatrick—who had previously earned the nickname "Kilcavalry"—lived up to his name that day. The 1st Vermont was decimated.

Experiences like this convinced U. S. Grant, when he took over the Federal forces eight months later, that the army needed a new chief of cavalry. He chose Major General Philip H. Sheridan, a short, slight, thirty-three-year-old infantry commander from the Western Theater, who was full of Irish temper and ferocity.

Grant wanted change and Sheridan, an infantryman, was unfettered by the outdated teachings of cavalry doctrine. Like Napoleon, Sheridan sought innovative ways of doing his job.

"I'm going to take this cavalry away from bobtailed brigadier generals. They must do without their escort," Sheridan warned. "I intend to make the cavalry an arm of the service."

Sheridan saw cavalry and infantry as a combined force. The job of the cavalry in his eyes was to use its mounts to advance the army's position faster and farther than men could march. Having reached such a strategic position, the cavalry would fight to hold the position until the infantry arrived.

Sheridan's troopers used both cavalry and infantry tactics. The mounted charge still had value, he reasoned, but only as an adjunct to men on the ground. Therefore, while the majority of Sheridan's men would dismount and fight as infantry, others would remain on horseback to exploit the gains of the men on the ground by attacking a breaking enemy line or pursuing a defeated foe. It was a powerful one-two punch.

Shortly after taking command, Sheridan had a run-in with the Army of the Potomac commander, George G. Meade, regarding the correct use of cavalry. Meade's imagination was limited. He believed the job of the cavalry was to support the infantry. Sheridan, on the other hand, saw his troopers as an integral part of a combined grand offensive.

Following the Battle of the Wilderness, Sheridan was so frustrated by Meade's constraints that he bucked their disagreement all the way up to Grant. The commanding general sided with Sheridan.

"I could whip Jeb Stuart," Sheridan boasted to Meade during one of their set-tos. For too long, Lee's young cavalry commander, Stuart, had been riding rings around (and usually whipping) Yankee horsemen. Grant's ruling gave Sheridan the opportunity he sought and he wasted no time in its implementation.

Sheridan set out with 10,000 cavalrymen into the rear of Lee's position protecting Richmond. Roaming around behind Lee's lines, Sheridan ripped up railroad tracks, destroyed over 100 railcars, a couple of locomotives, and most important, the rations for Lee's army.

"In just one day," wrote Shelby Foote in his classic *The Civil War*, "Sheridan had accomplished more than any of his predecessors had managed to do in the past three years."

Stuart's cavalry caught up with Sheridan on May 11, 1864, only six miles north of Richmond at a derelict old stagecoach inn known as Yellow Tavern. The Rebels—outmanned by better than two to one—took a concave defensive position that enabled them to pour a concentrated fire into any Yankee advance. After a couple of hours of probing, Sheridan sent Major General George Armstrong Custer (later of Little Big Horn fame) to attack the Rebel left.

It was cavalry versus cavalry, yet the majority of men were dismounted. Stuart's men were fighting from behind defensive positions. Custer's advance was half on foot and half on horseback.

Sheridan later described the clash as an "obstinate contest." The Rebels were unable to stop Sheridan. After a few hours of fighting, the Union force moved around the Graybacks and pushed on toward Richmond.

Not only had the Bluecoats not been stopped, but far worse, Jeb Stuart, the Virginia Cavalier, was fatally wounded by a Yankee bullet from a dismounted trooper.

Phil Sheridan had transformed the Union cavalry. Sometimes fighting as infantry, sometimes as horsemen, Sheridan had made his troopers into a strategic "arm of the service," just as he had envisioned.

Civil War Entrepreneur Embraces Change
THE LIGHTNING BRIGADE

Leaders unencumbered by outmoded military doctrine were often the Civil War's most effective innovators. Sheridan was successful, in part, because he didn't think like a cavalryman. Volunteer soldiers, too, operating on common sense and their own observations, were quite innovative.

While old-line generals still struggled with the impact of rifling grooves in the barrel of a musket, for instance, a number of young Civil War officers embraced an even newer innovation—the breech-loading, multiple-shot rifle—as a tool for the infantry.

Two repeater models—the Spencer seven-shot rifle and the Henry sixteen-shot rifle—were developed during the war. The Union army, however, failed to deploy the repeating rifle on a wide scale. They were issued to the cavalry, but the bureaucrats in the War Department were afraid that in the hands of the infantry, the multi-shot rifle would encourage the troops to waste ammunition. (A Civil War lesson widely emulated by narrow-visioned corporate bean counters!)

But, in the same way that some corporate desk captains bought and installed their own PC's long before their employers embraced the personal computer, resourceful Civil War troops used their own money to buy repeating rifles.

"Many soldiers bought Spencers and Henrys out of their own pockets, looking on them as a life-preserving investment," writes historian John MacDonald in his *Great Battles of the Civil War*. In fact, Connecticut industrialist Christopher Spencer took to the road, visiting Union encampments as a traveling salesman to hawk his multi-shot rifle directly to the troops.

Spencer reached the Tennessee front in March 1863, and found a receptive customer in Colonel John Wilder of the Army of the Cumberland. Wilder was a volunteer who had been an industrialist himself before the war and, thus, was unencumbered by backward-looking military dogma.

Colonel Wilder had already differentiated himself from tradition-bound army-think by mounting his infantry brigade on horseback. Wilder's soldiers would fight dismounted, as infantry, but the horses would get them to the scene of action faster than on foot.

Wilder equipped his men with the new Spencer repeaters—at their own expense. Using his business contacts back home in Indiana, he arranged a bank loan to finance the purchase of the Spencers. Each of his 1,500 men agreed to have money deducted from his pay to reimburse the commander and pay off the loan.

The result of marrying horse and multi-shot repeating rifles created the fastest-moving and most powerfully armed unit in the west, eventually known as the "Lightning Brigade."

Just one week before General Lee's disaster at Gettysburg, Colonel Wilder's "Lightning Brigade" used its repeating rifles to lead a Union breakout from a stalemated confrontation in mid-Tennessee. The Battle of Hoover's Gap, as it became known, was the beginning of the end of the Confederacy's hold in that theater of the war.

One of Wilder's officers vividly recalled the effect of the Spencer rifle on the charging Rebels:

"A terrible fire from the 'Spencers' causes the advancing regiment to reel and its colors fall to the ground, but in an instant their colors are up again and on they come, thinking to reach the battery before our guns can be reloaded . . . they didn't know we had the 'Spencers' and their charging yell was answered by another terrible volley, and another and another without cessation, until, the poor regiment was literally cut to pieces."

Colonel Wilder may not have had the strategic and tactical genius of General Lee, but he did have something Lee lacked— the willingness to embrace change. As a result, the engagements at Gettysburg and Hoover's Gap produced radically different outcomes.

Sheridan Runs Lee to Ground
THE FINAL DAYS

It is perhaps poetic justice that Union Major General Philip Sheridan ended up defeating Robert E. Lee's Army of Northern Virginia by using some of the most innovative tactics of the Civil War.

"It is greatly to Sheridan's credit," wrote Paddy Griffith in *Battle Tactics of the Civil War*, "that he . . . pressed his ideas upon his more traditionally-minded superiors."

For nine months Lee had been dug in at Petersburg, south of Richmond. Grant was determined to get him out of his fortifications by continually extending the Union line to the left, forcing Lee to stretch his already thinly manned position.

At some point, Grant knew, Lee would have to make a break for it—presumably heading south to join up with General Joseph

Johnston's 20,000-man army fighting Union General Sherman's march through the Carolinas.

To spearhead the final operation against Lee, Grant chose Sheridan—both for the speed of his cavalry and for his aggressiveness and innovation. In the year since he came east, Sheridan's responsibility had continually grown. Now, the general-in-chief was telling him, "I mean to end the business here," with Sheridan in the forefront of that effort.

In Sheridan's campaign the infantry, in a reversal of roles, would support the cavalry.

On March 29, 1865, Grant sent Sheridan to turn the Rebel right. The plan was, first, to take the small town of Dinwiddie Court House, about six miles from the end of Lee's line, then advance to a critical intersection on a major artery feeding Richmond called Five Forks, and from there proceed three more miles to cut the Southside railroad, a key to any Confederate withdrawal.

When Lee discovered this maneuver, he attacked (of course), sending 12,000 men under Major General George Pickett to stop Sheridan. The first day Pickett did just that, although he withdrew to Five Forks that night.

Sheridan—whose favorite instructions were, "Smash 'em up! Smash 'em up!"—smashed into the Rebels at Five Forks on April 1. Described as "the most decisive action of dismounted and mounted cavalry during the war," Sheridan's innovative tactics produced what James McPherson's *Battle Cry of Freedom* called "the most one-sided Union victory since the long campaign began eleven months earlier."

The main pressure—dismounted cavalry under command of Major General George Custer and Brigadier General Thomas Devin—came up the road from Dinwiddie. Right behind them were additional troopers, mounted and ready to pounce should developments warrant.

"At one time my entire command was dismounted and fighting as infantry," Custer wrote in his report. Devin's report added that one regiment "was ordered to keep . . . mounted and in readiness to charge should the enemy's lines be broken . . . As the works were carried [the mounted regiment] was ordered to charge . . . clearing the breastworks at a bound, and charging far in advance of the division."

Sheridan's other innovation that day was to have the infantry act in support of the cavalry. While Custer et al. kept the front busy, the V Infantry Corps attacked the Rebels' left flank. Confident in his troopers (and because he had relieved the infantry commander in mid-battle for a lack of aggressiveness), Sheridan rode among the infantry, driving them onward.

The troopers in front prevailed, as did the infantry on the flank. As the two forces converged jubilantly, Sheridan rode among them. Rising in his stirrups, he bellowed, "I want you men to understand we have a record to make before the sun goes down that will make hell tremble."

The diminutive general then pointed north in the direction of the Southside railroad. "I want you *there!*"

On Sunday, April 2, a courier walked down the aisle during the morning service at St. Paul's Church in Richmond and handed the President of the Confederacy, Jefferson Davis, a message. It was from Robert E. Lee—the lines had broken and the Southside railroad was cut. An ashen Davis departed immediately.

The next morning Yankees occupied Richmond. Forty hours after Jefferson Davis fled his Southern "White House," Abraham Lincoln was sitting in the former office of the President of the Confederate States of America.

For the next week, Phil Sheridan continued the Union chase of the Army of Northern Virginia. Choosing not to follow Lee and nip at his heels, Sheridan sought instead to get in front of the Rebels and bag them once and for all.

Lee kept moving westward, looking for an opportunity to turn the corner and head south. But as he moved, Sheridan's coordinated cavalry-infantry tactics decimated Lee's army. The rear half of the Rebel force had to stop frequently to fight off the Union cavalry. As a result, it became separated from Lee's front half. The cavalry broke Lee's army in two, leaving them prey to the Union infantry.

On Palm Sunday, April 9, 1865, Lee tried to break through Sheridan's troopers near Appomattox Court House. The Rebels drove the Union cavalry back, only to find the Federal infantry right behind. The Southern breakthrough failed. Robert E. Lee surrendered later that day.

Sheridan's innovative combination of cavalry and infantry working in unison produced a whole that was greater than the sum of the parts, had they been working independently. This new force stopped Lee from maneuvering away as he had so successfully done before.

The Army of Northern Virginia, led by the audacious, mobile, but noninnovative Robert E. Lee had been run to ground by the audacious, mobile, and highly innovative Philip Sheridan.

Corporate Commanders Confront Change
CIVIL WAR LESSONS APPLIED TO BUSINESS

How corporate leaders respond to changed circumstances can be as decisive in business today as it was for Lee and Sheridan.

The leader of Internet pioneer Netscape, James Barksdale, traces his roots to Confederate General William Barksdale, who was killed leading his brigade of Mississippians in a traditional head-on assault. Hanging in the modern Barksdale's office is a painting of his ancestor heading to his death while leading his men across the wheat field at Gettysburg.

Jim Barksdale was not about to make the same mistake as his ancestor. Confronting the massed legions of Microsoft's army in the Internet Browser Wars, he changed Netscape's business focus to avoid a head-on assault. Instead of marching into the sights of Microsoft's rifles to battle for the end-user browser market, Netscape sacrificed $50 million in annual revenue from end-user sales and recast itself as an on-line company.

Because the Netscape browser defaulted to the company's home page, Netscape was the World Wide Web's second most popular "portal." Each month 20 million people found their way on to the Internet through its Netcenter home page. As a result of this strategic metamorphosis, Netscape evolved from a browser company to an on-line media company. From this position Barksdale could hold his own high ground instead of assaulting Microsoft on the ground of its choosing.

Willing to embrace even the greatest of changes, Barksdale then brought in reinforcements by merging with America Online to create the dominant on-line electronic commerce presence. Jim Barksdale didn't just confront change—he embraced it.

Norman R. Augustine confronted a similar problem. Augustine was at the helm of Martin Marietta, a major defense contractor, just as the Cold War was ending and the defense industry was looking at a full 60 percent drop in Pentagon orders. This was bad news for Augustine and his fellow defense contractors. Their stark choice was similar to that Lee and Sheridan faced when they were confronted by the newfangled weapons—adapt or die.

As Augustine wrote in the *Harvard Business Review*, "There are only two kinds of companies—those that are changing and those that are going out of business."

The strategy adopted by Augustine was to increase his share of a declining market and raise margins by consolidating with competitors. The newly formed Lockheed Martin Corporation, with Augustine as chairman and CEO, ultimately comprised seventeen previously independent enterprises.

As a second part of the strategy, Lockheed Martin's production shifted away from the previous concentration on building aircraft mainframes to the fabrication of electronic and other high-tech upgrades, which, after all, are replaced more frequently than an entire airplane.

Lockheed Martin became the number-one provider to the Department of Defense, Department of Energy, and NASA. It is the world's leader in building satellites and the American leader in launching spacecraft.

Augustine cites his own nineteenth-century examples of enterprises that failed to adapt to change: "None of the companies that dominated the thriving ice-harvesting market converted to the refrigeration business. The Pony Express did not develop into a railroad."

While most managers are confronted with change on the magnitude of the Civil War or the end of the Cold War only once in decades or centuries, rapid changes in the computer industry seem to come daily or even hourly. The experience of two computer industry leaders proves Augustine's rule that a company that is not changing is a company that is dying.

Scott McNealy, CEO of Sun Microsystems, had a major problem in the mid-1990s—the market for Sun's individual workstations, powered by the UNIX operating system and the company's proprietary microprocessors, was about to be overtaken by network servers using Intel chips and Microsoft programs.

McNealy responded by changing the way he did business. Sun adjusted its product line to take advantage of the evolving server market, retrained its sales force from order-takers to systems integration solution providers, and acquired other innovative companies with ideas for meeting the expanding needs of its customers.

But to survive on the business battlefield, McNealy knew it is often necessary to guide change, not just react to it.

Instead of merely fending off the challenge to UNIX from Microsoft's Windows NT software, McNealy went on the offensive, promoting his Java programming language as the new and improved industry standard and as the solution for new applications. Suddenly with Java, *he* was the one introducing seminal change to the battlefield.

Digital Equipment Corporation's response to change sorely lacked such innovation. Digital and its CEO Ken Olsen had pioneered mini-computers and stolen a march on giant IBM. But, ultimately, Olsen became as intransigent as Lee at Gettysburg, failing to see and adapt to the changes around him.

The rise of Digital's mini-computers can be traced to a 1965 theory propounded by Gordon Moore, later a founder of chipmaker Intel. Moore's Law stated that the processing power of microchip technology would double every eighteen months while the cost fell by 50 percent . . . and would continue to do so indefinitely.

As Moore's Law made possible ever smaller and more powerful computers—personal computers—Digital's Ken Olsen refused to adapt his business to the new development by going after the home computer market.

In a classic example of frozen thinking, Olsen cracked, "Who would ever want one in his home?"

Belatedly Digital made a couple of forays into PCs, but its heart was never in it. And in 1998, Digital ceased to exist. Compaq, an enormously successful PC company that had been committed to adaptive change since its founding, acquired Digital, keeping what it wanted and discarding the rest.

The examples of business leaders' successful adaptations to change—or their tragic failure to do so—are endless.

Sears survived the retail revolution by retargeting its market to working mothers and offering value-priced, family-friendly apparel. Montgomery Ward, on the other hand, died because it saw the necessity of change too late and made the wrong strategic decisions.

Nokia—a Finnish company known previously for rubber boots and paper products—became the dominant force in cellular telephone handsets when its leaders saw an opportunity presented by the conversion from analog to digital wireless networks. Motorola, the previous world leader in wireless, did not move aggressively enough to embrace the new technology and, as a result, missed the market.

Charles Schwab, the brokerage company, built its niche as the "un-broker" for clients who didn't care about the services of traditional brokerages and only wanted a brokerage which would execute their stock transactions for a very low fee. When the Internet made stock transactions even cheaper, Schwab changed tactics.

"We can't build a business on trading anymore," a Schwab executive told *Business Week*, "because that service is a commodity."

The old Schwab, therefore, changed. The "un-broker" became the personal discount broker, hanging on to its clients through new offerings built on personal attention (as opposed to the impersonal Internet). Far from being threatened, Schwab grew.

Marching Orders

Civil War historian Bruce Catton wrote in *America Goes to War*: "It took the generals a long time to adjust themselves to the change [in weaponry] which had occurred while the war was going on . . . Many of the tragedies and apparent blunders in that war came simply because the generals were trained in tactics which were worse than useless."

The rifled musket existed for fifteen years before Robert E. Lee, following his defeat at Gettysburg, belatedly began adapting to the defensive strategy it required. The speed of change in today's Information Age denies current business leaders the luxury of such a leisurely timetable.

Microsoft CEO Bill Gates says, "One of the toughest parts of managing, especially in a high-tech business, is to recognize the need for change, and make it while you still have a chance . . . when change is inevitable, you must spot it, embrace it, and find ways to make it work for you."

As it was in the Civil War, the imperative today is to adapt or die.

Lesson Four

It's the Next Hill

Grasping the true scope of the battle is as important as fighting it

The battle is never over.

It is the responsibility of each leader to keep his or her troops moving forward, to overcome the natural human desire to declare victory and rest on the day's laurels.

Great leaders see beyond individual battles to the entire conflict, and make their decisions accordingly.

The Union lost the first major battle of the war, First Manassas (Bull Run), because the commanding general took the first hill on the battlefield and stopped. Contrary to that experience, Robert E. Lee saved Richmond in 1862 by seeing beyond individual defeats and pushing for the larger strategic goal, the figurative next hill.

The outcome of the greatest battle ever fought in America, Gettysburg, was determined in large measure on its first day, when a Confederate general failed to exploit his victory and press on to secure the next hill in front of him.

The ultimate victory belongs to the leader who is able to continually reassess the scope of the conflict and keep pushing on to the next hill.

Looking Beyond the First Hill
FIRST MANASSAS (BULL RUN), 1861

In April of 1861, President Lincoln called for 75,000 volunteer soldiers to serve for ninety days, on the assumption that the Southern rebellion would be stamped out quickly. As the expiration of those short-term enlistments approached, without a single major engagement against the secessionists having been fought, the demand "On to Richmond" rose in the Northern press and among elected Federal officials.

Brigadier General Irvin McDowell, a careful organizer and planner, was chosen to lead the Union advance against the Confederate capital a mere 100 miles from Washington. But the forty-two-year-old Ohioian, schooled at West Point and tested in the Mexican War, complained that his troops were too inexperienced for battle and needed additional training.

Lincoln dismissed his concerns: "You are green. The Rebels are green. You are all green alike."

The Confederates chose not to defend the Virginia countryside immediately across the Potomac from Washington, but rather to concentrate their defenses slightly more than twenty miles away at a point between Washington and Richmond called Manassas Junction. There two strategic rail lines crossed—one leading south toward the Confederate capital, the other through a gap in the Blue Ridge Mountains to the Shenandoah Valley.

The Shenandoah was Virginia's breadbasket, as well as a sheltered pathway through the heartland of the state leading from the outskirts of Washington to the back door of Richmond.

Commanding the Confederates at Manassas was the victor of

Fort Sumter, General P. G. T. Beauregard. A classmate of Mc-Dowell's at West Point, this short, fit Creole had gone on to become superintendent of the military academy.

At Beauregard's immediate disposal were 23,000 Rebel soldiers. Through the gap in the Blue Ridge Mountains, the second part of the Confederate army, 15,000 men in the Shenandoah Valley, was positioned under the command of General Joseph Johnston, another veteran of the Mexican War.

McDowell's plan was to use his 35,000 Federal troops to push past Manassas, force his way through the gap in the Blue Ridge, and sweep into the Shenandoah Valley to defeat Johnston's force there.

Outside of Manassas, between the Federal troops and Beauregard's men, ran a natural obstacle, a small creek with steep banks—Bull Run. Dominated by high ground and crossed only by three fords and a stone bridge, Bull Run became the cornerstone of the Confederate strategy.

On July 16, 1861, McDowell's army departed Washington for Manassas. The newspapers conveniently covered his advance. Southern sympathizers in the capital made sure those helpful intelligence reports—complete with maps—were soon in General Beauregard's hands.

The twenty-mile Yankee march to Centreville, the staging ground, illustrated just how inexperienced McDowell's army was. Later in the war, troops would cover this distance, and more, in a day. But in 1861, it took two days for the green army's advance guard to reach the vicinity of Bull Run. Not until July 21 did McDowell feel prepared to launch his attack.

While McDowell was marching, Johnston's Confederates in the Shenandoah had given the slip to the Union troops charged with keeping them bottled up in the valley. In a historic first, the Rebel troops embarked on railroad trains that would carry them directly to the battlefield at Manassas.

The battle would be decided by whether or not Beauregard

could hold out against McDowell's numerical superiority until Johnston's troops arrived.

Ironically, McDowell and Beauregard each had a plan of attack set for the same day that was a mirror image of the other's. Each would attack the other's left flank. But McDowell struck first, having awakened his men at 2 A.M. to march through the darkness and cross Bull Run at a lightly protected ford far beyond the Rebel flank.

It was a good plan. Beauregard had weakened his left flank in order to mount an attack to his right. This meant that when the Union assault began around 10 A.M., the Federals had overwhelming numerical superiority on their chosen battleground. Despite a stiff defense by the Rebs, McDowell captured his objective, Matthews Hill, by around noon.

The Confederates retreated to the next high ground on the battlefield—known as Henry Hill after the residence of the Widow Henry (who was mortally wounded in the fighting that day).

By bringing his flanking force through the Confederate opposition to occupy Matthews Hill, McDowell was reunited with the main body of his troops on the other side of Bull Run. He not only had driven the Rebels from Matthews Hill, he now also controlled the anchor point of the Rebels' defense, the fords and the bridge over the stream.

The Union commander rode along his line of soldiers, waving his hat and shouting, "Victory! Victory! The day is ours!"

An engineer was sent to telegraph the good news to Lincoln.

But the claim of victory was premature. Unable to see behind Henry Hill, either literally or metaphorically, McDowell shortsightedly declared the battle over. It wasn't. McDowell's well-planned and well-executed attack was to be wasted by his overly optimistic interpretation of the tide of events—his inability to grasp the full scope of the battle in which he was engaged.

While Lincoln went for a carriage ride to relax after receiving his commander's "victory" telegram, General Beauregard, the Confederate general, redeployed his men to attack, bringing back those soldiers he had dispatched on the now-aborted mission against the Union left flank. Johnston's troops from the Shenandoah Valley, too, were at last piling off their trains and moving into battle formation.

After taking Matthews Hill and declaring victory, McDowell stopped his pursuit of the Rebels. Two hours passed before he went on the offensive again—and then only by firing off his artillery. The Confederates responded with their own artillery barrage, grateful for the long-range engagement since there were still only 3,000 Confederates on Henry Hill.

Following a one-hour bombardment, McDowell finally ordered his infantry to attack the Rebels on the hill. But instead of a general advance using his advantage in numbers, the Federal commander, still not imagining the battle's scope, sent his units in piecemeal.

For the next two hours, the fighting seesawed back and forth. One battery of Union artillery, for instance, was taken by the Rebels, retaken, and then lost again. The home-sewn mismatched uniforms of each side added to the confusion as some Union troops dressed in gray were mistaken for Rebels and Confederates dressed in blue were mistaken for Union soldiers.

During those hours of chaos and gunfire on Henry Hill, a former Virginia Military Institute professor, Brigadier General Thomas J. Jackson, acquired his immortal nickname.

Jackson's brigade was almost all that stood between McDowell and the Confederate rear and the Virginians weren't budging. Another Confederate general called out to his men, "There is Jackson standing like a stone wall! Let us determine to die here, and we will conquer."

"Stonewell" Jackson held his ground and became the rallying point on Henry Hill.

As the afternoon wore on, more and more Confederates from

the Shenandoah Valley flooded onto the battlefield, finally turning the tide.

Beauregard did not repeat McDowell's mistake of sending his men into battle in small parts. Strengthened by the troops from the trains, Beauregard ordered his entire line of battle to charge forward. Across the high ground of Henry Hill, down into the valley between Henry and Matthews hills, across Bull Run, the Confederates chased the Union troops.

The glorious Union victory became a Union rout. Panic rippled through the Federals. The green troops became a scared mob.

Confederate Colonel Jubal Early observed, "We scared the enemy worse than we hurt him."

McDowell's after-battle report described the scene: "The plain was covered with the retreating troops, and they seemed to infect those with whom they came in contact. The retreat soon became a rout, and this soon degenerated still further into a panic." The Federal troops fled all the way back to Washington.

President Lincoln came home from his celebratory carriage ride to find another telegram. "General McDowell's army is in full retreat . . . The day is lost. Save Washington and the remnants of this army."

Had McDowell seen the battle's full scope, instead of a too-early snapshot, he would have pushed on and captured Henry Hill when he held the advantage. Then the day would have been won instead of lost for the Federals.

Despite Defeats, Lee Continues to Push to the "Next Hill"
THE SEVEN DAYS, 1862

Eleven months after the battle at Manassas, Robert E. Lee took command of Confederate forces in Virginia. Far from the victorious experience along Bull Run, Lee inherited a command with its back to the wall. The Union army was at the gates of Richmond, vastly outnumbering the defenders.

The key to any success, Lee realized, was to deny the initiative to the Union by maintaining the initiative himself. This meant always going for the next hill, even when to do so many have seemed imprudent.

In the Seven Days' Battles that ultimately drove the Union troops away from Richmond, Lee kept pressing for the "next hill" even when he wasn't winning. The Confederates lost all but one of the battles during those seven days. Yet, because Lee's strategic vision exceeded any one specific engagement, his pursuit of that vision—even in the face of plans that went awry and horrific losses—resulted in a major victory.

The first of the Seven Days' Battles, June 25, 1862, was a Confederate defeat, the Battle of Oak Grove. In that small-scale engagement, Union troops were successful in advancing their picket lines to test the Confederate position.

The following day Lee planned a relatively uncomplicated maneuver. The majority of his troops would be concentrated against the weakest point of the Union position, the V Corps, isolated on the north side of the Chickahominy River. Troops of Major General A. P. Hill's division were to attack the front while Stonewall Jackson's men would hit the Union flank.

Jackson, however, was a phantom. Hill's troops waited until late in the afternoon for word that Jackson was ready. When he never showed up, they attacked anyway, chased a small number of Bluecoats from their position at Mechanicsville, and then fell into a buzzsaw of Union troops entrenched along Beaver Dam Creek.

Lee's generalship was undistinguished. Of the 56,000 troops at his disposal, only 14,000 were used and (shades of McDowell) those were brought to bear incrementally. The second day, too, was won by the Union army.

That night Union commander Major General George B. Mc-

Clellan withdrew his troops four miles to the rear, establishing his line on high ground behind another creek just south of the mill on Dr. Gaines' plantation.

The following day, Lee attacked the Union position. Again, the assault was poorly executed—Lee sent one division in a frontal assault against a foe that was twice its number, in anticipation that Stonewall Jackson would assault the flank. But again, there was no action from Stonewall's side of the field.

Finally, late in the afternoon Jackson's troops attacked. Tired and stretched out, the Union line broke at the end of the day and Bluecoats fled to the rear. Lee had finally produced a victory, despite rampant mismanagement among his subordinates.

On the fourth day, the combatants licked their wounds. Lee—outmanned and outequipped—used the time to plan another assault. McClellan used it to prepare a withdrawal.

On June 29—day five—the Rebels attacked the rear guard of the Federal retreat. But the battle of Savage's Station ended with another Confederate loss.

The sixth day was still another Southern fiasco. Lee planned a double envelopment with troops descending on both Union flanks. But his troops never showed up. Finally, around five o'clock, with President Jefferson Davis (a West Point graduate, veteran of the Mexican War, and former U.S. Secretary of War) looking on (and no doubt kibitzing), Lee ordered an attack.

Fortunately, this ragtag assault was shortly put out of its misery by darkness. Once more the Confederates had not been stymied.

The climax of Lee's tactical failures occurred on the seventh day, July 1, 1862, at Malvern Hill.

"Had the Union engineers searched the whole countryside below Richmond, they could not have found ground more ideally suited for slaughter of an enemy army," wrote one observer. One side of the hill was creeks and cliffs; the other was not only steep but also under the guns of the Union warships anchored on the James River. The only assault path was straight up the middle.

Looking down on the assault path from atop Malvern Hill sat massed Union artillery. When loaded with canister shells their effect was like gigantic shotguns that would mow down the advancing troops.

To knock out these batteries, Lee ordered a grand artillery bombardment from his own guns. Far fewer in number, the Rebel cannon failed in their assigned task. In the afternoon, mistakenly believing the Federals were retreating, the Confederate troops surged forward into the sure hell of the Union cannon.

"It wasn't war," wrote Confederate General D. H. Hill, "it was murder."

In seven days of continuous fighting, Robert E. Lee's forces had prevailed only once. Yet his strategic victory was complete.

Lee had kept pushing, pursuing an expansive vision, despite losing all but one of the engagements. This constant expansion of the scope of the conflict intimidated, harassed, and disoriented his opposition. After Malvern Hill, the Union troops withdrew another eight miles to a secure position at Harrison's Landing. Eventually the invaders withdrew from southern Virginia altogether.

Handed command of the Southern army in the worst of circumstances, Lee prevailed because he defined the scope of his effort, not in terms of individual battles, but as a broader objective—defending Richmond and taking the initiative from his opponent by always pushing for the "next hill."

The Hill That Decided the Greatest Battle
GETTYSBURG, DAY ONE, 1863

The greatest battle ever fought on American soil, Gettysburg, lasted for three days. The Gettysburg of popular memory is the battle of the second and third days—Confederate troops vainly attempting to drive Union forces from the heights south of the small Pennsylvania town, culminating in Pickett's ill-fated charge (see Lesson Three).

However, it was the first day, July 1, 1863, which determined the battle's outcome, the ultimate Union victory—even though it was the Confederates who were the victors on that first day.

Under Stonewall Jackson, the II Corps had set the pace for the Rebel army. On the move, the II Corps marched the fastest among the Confederate troops. On the battlefield, it was Lee's favorite offensive punch. And within the II Corps, Richard Ewell's division was the one to which Jackson looked to set the pace. As a result, after the death of Jackson two months before Gettysburg (see Lesson Five), Robert E. Lee promoted Ewell to command the II Corps.

On the first day of the battle, it was no surprise that the II Corps, now under Ewell's command, arrived at a key moment and fell upon the Union flank, driving the Federals back through the town of Gettysburg.

What was a surprise was what the II Corps did not do afterward when it failed to occupy the hills to the south of the town.

Richard Ewell was a brave general. The previous August he had lost a leg in battle, and he now hobbled about on a wooden leg. On the opening day of battle at Gettysburg, he had his horse shot out from under him in the morning and his wooden leg hit by a bullet in the afternoon. So it was certainly not lack of courage that caused Ewell to pull up short of the strategic hills overlooking Gettysburg.

The fact was, Ewell was struggling with his new responsibilities. Earlier in the day, he had shown his willingness to make a decision contrary to the wishes of his commanding general when he attacked while Lee was counseling caution. By the afternoon, however, the new corps commander had lost his nerve, just when Lee needed it most.

The Battle of Gettysburg was played out with the Southern forces arriving from the north and the Northern forces from the south. The clash on that first day took place to the north and west of the town. By 4:30 P.M., the Union troops were fleeing back through Gettysburg to shelter behind two hills beyond the city.

A little less than a mile south of Gettysburg lies Cemetery Hill, named for its principal occupants. Extending southward from the hill is a ridgeline, appropriately called Cemetery Ridge, where much of the next two days' fighting would be concentrated. To the east of Cemetery Hill, about half a mile further out of town, is Culp's Hill, rocky, wooded, and slightly higher than the adjoining promontories.

By controlling Culp's Hill, an army would control Cemetery Hill and the ridge, and thereby control the Gettysburg battlefield.

Robert E. Lee sent orders to General Ewell stating, "The enemy [is] retreating over those hills . . . in great confusion. You only need to press those people to secure possession of the heights . . . Do this, if practicable."

Lee's orders arrived following a spirited debate at Ewell's headquarters about just such a pursuit. Major General John B. Gordon had gone to the headquarters in hopes of being directed to attack Culp's Hill. Instead, he was met by silence from his corps commander. Lee's phrase, "if practicable" gave the uncertain Ewell an excuse not to act.

Another officer, Major General Isaac Trimble, pointing at Culp's Hill, exhorted Ewell, "General, there is an eminence of commanding position, and not now occupied . . . I advise you to send a brigade to hold it if we are to remain here."

When Ewell declined, legend recounts that Trimble urged, "Give me a brigade and I will engage to take that hill." Still receiving no positive reply, Trimble reduced the size of the force requested and removed the uncertainty. "Give me a regiment and I will do it."

As Ewell continued to dither, one of Stonewall Jackson's former staff commented to a fellow officer, "Oh, for the presence and inspiration of 'Old Jack' for just one hour!"

But "Old Jack" was dead. Ewell, worried about reports of Bluecoats on his left and rear and, perhaps, worried as well about the consequences of going against Lee's counsel of caution earlier in the day, chose to await further instructions.

In lieu of taking responsibility for deciding to take the hill on his own, Ewell dispatched a messenger to Lee suggesting that an attack on the hills was appropriate, but by the III Corps, the other Confederate force engaged in the day's fighting.

As dusk approached, Lee himself arrived at Ewell's headquarters. By then, nearly four hours of daylight had been frittered away. The major fighting for the day was over, the generals decided.

After Lee's departure, however, staff officers returned with reports that they had been on Culp's Hill and found it was still unoccupied by the Federals. With this information in hand, Ewell rode to Lee, requested and received permission to attack the hill.

Finally, in darkness, a newly arrived Confederate division was sent up Culp's Hill to occupy it. But by then it was too late. In the interim, the hill had been taken by Federal troops, who drove back the Confederates.

If Ewell had possessed the vision to press on to that next hill in the bright sunshine of a victorious afternoon, it could have changed the course of the Gettysburg battle.

Discussing Gettysburg three months before his death, Lee commented, "Ewell was a fine officer, but would never take the responsibility of exceeding his orders, and having been ordered to Gettysburg, he would not go farther and hold the heights beyond the town."

As historian Douglas Southall Freeman eloquently explained to the Army War College, the failure to take Culp's Hill "cost the

Confederates Cemetery Hill, and Cemetery Hill cost them Cemetery Ridge, and Cemetery Ridge cost them Gettysburg. What Gettysburg cost them, you know."

The Same Mistakes—132 Years Later
DISNEY LOSES THE "THIRD BATTLE OF MANASSAS"

The routes which made the crossroads of Manassas, Virginia, strategically important and twice drew Union and Confederate troops into battle for its control were no less valuable in the twentieth century.

Thoroughfare Gap, cutting through the Blue Ridge Mountains, now carries Interstate Highway 66. Warrenton Pike, the route from Washington over which General McDowell's troops advanced and then retreated, is now Route 29. These transportation arteries made the land around Manassas as commercially attractive in the late twentieth century as it was militarily important in the mid-nineteenth century.

In 1973, the Marriott Corporation proposed to build a "Great America" theme park at Manassas. In 1986, a local developer tried to build an office park and shopping mall in proximity to the battlefield. Both proposals were defeated by antidevelopment and historic preservation coalitions.

In 1993, the Walt Disney Company—an icon of American business and popular culture—determined that the Manassas crossroads would be the ideal site for its third theme park, "Disney's America," a celebration of America's heritage amid Virginia's many historic sites and close to the tourist Mecca of Washington, D.C.

For two years, Disney surreptitiously bought significant plots of land less than four miles from the battlefield. Using multiple realtors and anonymous surrogates, such as Peachtree Land Corp. and Carter Beef Co., Disney assembled 3,000 acres for the theme park, hotels, golf courses, and shops. Disney was prepared to invest $650 million, hire 3,000 people and pay (over thirty years) $1.5 billion in taxes.

The same formula which Walt Disney had used in the creation of the original Disneyland in California was applied again—pick a site that is big, cheap, close to highways, and within the boundaries of a friendly government which is susceptible to economic blandishments.

Disney's quiet offensive was a masterpiece of planning and implementation. Yet, it failed for precisely the same reason General Irvin McDowell failed on the same ground more than 130 years earlier.

Disney misjudged the true scope of its battle.

On November 11, 1993, Disney rocked the national capital region with the public announcement of "Disney's America," which would re-create and dramatize important events of the country's history.

The *Washington Post* characterized the venture as a "catalyst for investment in western Prince William County." The county's economic development director crowed, "It proves that if you work hard you can be rewarded."

Within days of the Disney announcement, the Piedmont Environmental Council drew 450 people to the Episcopal church in The Plains, Virginia, to organize opposition to Disney's plan. These homegrown activists would take on the Great American Company and the machine it had quietly assembled to steamroller such opposition.

The county government supported the theme park, as did Virginia's new governor. It seemed as though everyone was in Disney's corner. Fifteen lobbyists registered for Disney in Richmond to lobby the state legislature to approve the governor's request for $163 million in infrastructure support.

"Disney has hired some of the most familiar faces in Richmond to make its case," the *Washington Post* observed. "The lobbyists are well connected, they are experienced, and they are everywhere.''

Behind this team was an army of pollsters, media consultants, telemarketers, economists, and other arm-twisters and spin doctors.

Disney's plan of battle was superb and well executed—a surprise attack emphasizing the fabulous economic benefits of the theme park followed by repeated assaults with studies and PR to blunt the opposition. Disney's deep-pocketed army would simply wear down and then roll over the opponents.

"Our intention is to continue our process of education and communication so that by the end . . . we're going to be able to allay almost all private fears and concerns," Disney's spokesman explained.

At first, the anti-Disney response was as predicted. Arguments about urban sprawl, the threat of higher taxes and traffic congestion were the weapons of the counter-attack. Disney had anticipated this strategy by its opponents and was prepared to assail it.

Like McDowell, Disney had a good plan and the plan was prevailing.

Then, amid the anticipated rhetoric about sprawl and overdevelopment, there surfaced a new rallying cry from the pen of Richard Moe, head of the National Trust for Historic Preservation and author of a Civil War history. In a *Washington Post* commentary, Moe asked what Disney's ersatz history would mean to the "authentic historic sites" in the area.

More significantly, he asked, "What will 'Disney's America' mean for the teaching of American history?"

These words offered the opposition a new and savvy political strategy for fighting Disney. Behind the counter-attack were two experienced political strategists: Moe himself, who had previously served as chief of staff to Vice President Walter Mondale, and the Piedmont Environmental Council's unofficial adviser, Julian Scheer, the man selected by President Kennedy to create the favorable national image for the Apollo man-on-the-moon project.

Although fresh troops were massing behind Henry Hill, the Disney forces barely noticed. As unaware of its opponents' new strategy and the consequences as McDowell had been on the same Virginia land 132 years earlier, Disney kept right on fighting the old battle, assuming that its campaign of smug reassurances and economic blandishments would assure victory.

Even months after Moe's newspaper column should have sounded a warning, Disney stuck to its old strategy by sweetening the deal. Disney upped the ante by offering to give the local government seventy-three acres for two public schools, a library, a fire station, and twenty sports fields.

Then the opponents fired their big guns and redefined the battle.

At a Washington news conference organized by Protect Historic America, a new Scheer-inspired organization, five big-name guardians of America's past—noted historians David McCullough, James McPherson, Shelby Foote, Doris Kearns Goodwin, and Arthur Schlesinger, Jr.—condemned Disney as the destroyer of our heritage.

"The ghosts of battles past, of patriots past . . . have transformed the conflict into far more than a local land-use issue or even a regional debate over traffic congestion and air pollution," the *Washington Post* noted insightfully.

David McCullough, known to millions from his frequent scholarly appearances on PBS, set the tone for the new attack by declaring that "Disney's America" would "create synthetic history by destroying real history" and replace it with "plastic, contrived history, mechanical history."

Not only had the opponents redefined Disney's fight for its theme park as a debate over America's heritage, they also charged that "Disney's America" would threaten an entire region's thirteen historic towns, sixteen Civil War battle sites, and seventeen historic districts, including Thomas Jefferson's home, Monticello, sixty miles away.

Disney's theme park "would desecrate the ground over which men fought and died for principles of enduring importance," argued Pulitzer Prize winner James McPherson.

Disney officials, secure in the false confidence that their strategy of stealth and influence would win the battle against such emotion-laden appeals, could only respond snidely, "It is unfortunate that a group of historians would prejudge the 'Disney America' project and draw conclusions . . . without having the necessary facts." An adequate response for a local land-use fight, perhaps, but totally inadequate in response to the assertion of historical desecration in what was now a national debate.

The outcome of the battle was sealed three weeks after the historians' press conference when Disney Chairman Michael Eisner appeared on "CBS This Morning" to defend his company's plan. The debate had moved on to the next hill and was now national news. Eisner, however, saw only the first hill and continued to treat the discussion as a local story.

In response to a question about turning the historic Virginia countryside into the plastic excess of Orlando, Eisner cluelessly responded that residents of the historic area "should be so lucky as to have Orlando in Virginia."

In a subsequent session with *Washington Post* editors, Eisner acknowledged that he had underestimated his opponents. If he had foreseen the ferocity of the opposition, he would have delayed the project and taken more time to prepare a public relations campaign, Eisner said.

In other words, the commanding general admitted that he had misjudged the scope of the battle. Eisner was conceding that Disney's battle plan was designed to take the first hill—a contest defined by traditional land development strategies—and was unprepared for the more critical battle on the hill of historic heritage.

Eisner quipped, "The First Amendment gives you the right to be plastic . . . We have a right to do it. It's private land that is not in the middle of an historic area . . . It's not in the middle of a battlefield."

Three months after the historians joined the opposition, after the county had approved the Disney rezoning, and after state and regional authorities had funded the highway improvements, the counter-attack from the next hill achieved its goal.

Weary of the continual pummeling, Michael Eisner took to the Disney board of directors a draft press release announcing the cancellation of "Disney's America." The board unanimously approved the cancellation.

With a justified twist of irony, Richard Moe praised Eisner and Disney as "patriots."

Marching Orders

"History is full of tragic accounts of campaigns lost because leaders stopped on the wrong side of the river, because they didn't have the initiative to exploit the advantage of the battle just won, and because they failed to obey the basic requirement to constantly be on the offensive," wrote World War II General George S. Patton.

Union General Irvin McDowell and Confederate General Richard Ewell proved Patton's admonition and forever will suffer in history.

Robert E. Lee is revered as a great leader precisely because he was always pressing on to the next hill.

Long before the Civil War, the book of *Proverbs* articulated and defined a basic leadership truth: "Where there is no vision, the people perish."

Lesson Five

A Bold Response Can Trump a Perfect Plan

Audacity

In business as in war, one must strive to force your opponent to respond to you.

To Napoleon, success in war required, "*L'audace, l'audace, toujours l'audace.*" Audacity, audacity, always audacity. The American Napoleon in this regard was Thomas Jonathan "Stonewall" Jackson. To Jackson fell the implementation of many of Robert E. Lee's creative and bold strategies.

Outmanned and outsupplied, the Lee–Jackson battlefield duo nevertheless practiced a boldness that forced their opponents into a responsive posture. As a result, the two Confederate generals prevailed in virtually every battle in which they jointly participated.

A leader is not timid. His or her audacity can deliver otherwise unattainable victories. Boldness is a trump card a leader must always be ready to play.

Audacity Spooks "Fighting Joe" Hooker
CHANCELLORSVILLE, 1863

After another Union debacle in December 1862, at Fredericksburg, Virginia, President Lincoln named Major General Joseph Hooker to command the Army of the Potomac, an appointment the general had schemed to attain. Aggressive in battle and vainglorious in person, "Fighting Joe" Hooker believed a military dictatorship was essential if the North was to win the war.

In his typically direct manner, Lincoln told his new field commander, "It was not for this [advocacy of a dictatorship], but in spite of it, that I have given you the command. Only those generals who gain successes can set up as dictators. What I now ask of you is military success, and I will risk the dictatorship."

In late January 1863, Hooker began rebuilding a Federal army that had been shattered by too many defeats under the supervision of a string of timid commanders. Under the new commander, food and sanitary conditions improved and illness among the troops decreased. Furloughs were granted in units that had performed well. Whiskey was allotted to soldiers when they returned from picket duty.

The Army of the Potomac under Hooker was the largest fighting force yet assembled in the Civil War. Recruitment had swelled its ranks to 134,000 men at arms, divided into seven corps.

In one of his most innovative improvements, Hooker instituted distinctive insignia for each corps. The effect upon morale of these symbols on a soldier's uniform was quite remarkable. To this day, unit pride is created and competition stirred by Hooker's innovation of displaying insignia on military uniforms.

Facing Hooker across the Rappahannock River in the spring of 1863, about halfway between Washington and Richmond, was the Confederate Army of Northern Virginia, commanded by Robert E. Lee. Lee's force was less than half the number on the Union side.

Hooker wasted no time in planning to go on the offensive. Within three months of assuming command, his army was in motion.

"My plans are perfect," Hooker told his officers with typical immodesty, "and when I start to carry them out, may God have mercy on General Lee, for I will have none."

Hooker's plan *did* seem perfect and its early execution was virtually flawless.

While feinting an attack below Fredericksburg with 40,000 men, Hooker sent three Union corps of 42,000 troops marching northwest across the Rappahannock far beyond the fords guarded by the Rebels. When this Union flanking force turned south, Lee would be trapped in the jaws of a vise. Hooker would need only to close the jaws to crush the Confederate army.

By April 30, 1863, Hooker had executed his flanking maneuver, and Robert E. Lee wasn't even aware that Hooker's forces were closing in on him from behind.

"Hurrah for old Joe," Union General Meade wrote to a subordinate. "We are now on Lee's flank, and he does not know it."

In a congratulatory message to his troops Hooker proclaimed, "Our enemy must either ingloriously fly, or come out from behind his defenses and give us battle on our own ground, where certain destruction awaits him."

"I have the rebellion in my breeches pocket, and God almighty himself cannot take it away from me," Hooker boasted. "The rebel army is now the legitimate property of the Army of the

Potomac. They may as well pack up their haversacks and make for Richmond. I shall be after them."

The logical action for a commander who discovers his outnumbered force is trapped in a vise would be to try to slip out the side and regroup at a more tactically feasible position.

Lee, however, decided to go on the offensive. *L'audace, l'audace, toujours l'audace.*

"It was now apparent," Lee wrote, "that the main attack would be made upon our flank and rear. It was therefore determined to leave sufficient troops to hold our lines [at Fredericksburg], and with the main body of the army to give battle to the approaching column."

This understated report fails to convey the magnitude of Lee's decision. He was not just giving battle to the approaching Federal column; he was violating one of the basic maxims of war by dividing his troops in the face of superior numbers.

Leaving 9,000 men in gray to deal with the 40,000 Union troops of Hooker's feinting force south of Fredericksburg, Lee sent the remainder of his troops to confront the main body of bluecoats, now grown to 70,000, advancing on his rear.

By early the following day, May 1, Stonewall Jackson's corps had arrived to join Lee's troops. Jackson's men brought the total number of Confederates on the field up to around 41,000, still less than 60 percent of the Union soldiers in Hooker's pincer closing in from behind.

When Jackson reached the scene of the impending battle, he found that Rebel troops who had arrived earlier were dug in atop a ridge. However, Jackson had no intention of going on the defensive. Stonewall ordered the men to get out of their trenches and march toward Hooker's advancing Union columns.

Advancing down the same road toward each other, the two forces clashed at 11:15 A.M.

The Southern troops struggled unsuccessfully to overcome the superior numbers of Hooker's force. Inexplicably, however, at around 2:00 P.M., Hooker ordered his troops to fall back to the Chancellor Inn, which gave the crossroads its name, Chancellorsville.

Lee's audacious and aggressive response to the "perfect" Union plan had intimidated Fighting Joe.

Despite overwhelming numerical and tactical superiority, the Union troops were on the defensive. Forming a convex line, centered at the Chancellorsville crossroads, Hooker awaited Lee's next move.

"The major general commanding trusts that a suspension in the attack to-day will embolden the enemy to attack him," Hooker lamely messaged his corps commanders. Talk about rationalization!

The "perfect" plan had initially resulted in exactly the outcome desired. Lee was caught by surprise and was forced to divide his outnumbered troops. Yet Hooker, the author of the plan, failed to seize his opportunity.

Robert E. Lee would not make the same mistake.

Late on the evening of May 1, Jackson and Lee met behind their lines, only about a mile south of Hooker's headquarters, to discuss tactics.

Lee had personally reconnoitered the Union left flank and found it secure. The center, likewise, was tight and dug in. Cavalry reports, however, indicated that the Union right was "hanging" in the open, detached and isolated from the main Federal battleline.

Lee decided to split his forces yet again.

The Confederate commander ordered Jackson to take 28,000 men, march twelve miles and fall upon Hooker's exposed right flank. Lee would stay with 13,000 men spread thinly across a three and a half mile front and try to keep Hooker busy.

The boldness and audacity of Lee's decision echoes as one of the most brilliant military maneuvers in history.

At the original point of contact near Fredericksburg, Lee still had 9,000 men holding off 40,000 Union troops. Around the Chancellorsville crossroads, Lee confronted another 70,000 bluecoats with only 13,000 Rebel soldiers. And now Lee was sending his largest force away from both Confederate groups, across the enemy's front, in a bold flanking movement.

The Army of Northern Virginia, already small but now deliberately split into three smaller parts, was ripe to be picked off piece by piece.

But Joe Hooker was not an audacious leader like Lee. Early on the morning of May 2, the Union commander saw Jackson's movement for himself through field glasses. He warned General Oliver Howard, commanding the right flank, to be on the alert.

Hooker, however, failed to take advantage of the obvious— that Lee's troops were now split into three small, disconnected units and, therefore, highly vulnerable to Union attack.

It took almost all day for Jackson's flank march to reach its destination. At 5:15 P.M., Stonewall Jackson fell upon the Union right. The result, determined in the first twenty minutes, was a rout of the Federals.

By 7 P.M. all resistance had collapsed and only nightfall kept Jackson from capturing the river fords in Hooker's rear—the Union route of retreat—which would have placed the Federal commander in the same kind of vise he had envisioned for Lee.

Even such a brilliantly executed response, however, had not assured a total Confederate victory. Lee's forces were split by Union troops occupying an area of high ground called Hazel Grove. Incredibly, instead of using Hazel Grove as the jumping-off point from which to attack the separated elements of the Confederate army, Hooker withdrew, thus allowing Lee to link his forces.

With his forces reunited—what else?—Lee went on the offensive.

Using the captured high ground of Hazel Grove as a base for

thirty-one Confederate artillery pieces, Lee bombarded the crumbling and confused Union positions. One Rebel shell struck Chancellor Inn, which was Hooker's headquarters, bringing down part of a pillar on the Union commander.

The Federals had one last chance to retrieve the victory that Hooker had so confidently predicted his "perfect" plan would achieve. The bottom part of the original Union vise in which Hooker had intended to squeeze Lee was still in place at Fredericksburg, and now began closing on the men in gray.

Lee's response should not have surprised anyone who had been watching him during those first days of May 1863. He split his forces one more time and went on the offensive. Lee pulled 10,000 men off the line at Chancellorsville and marched back toward the pincer of the Union vise from whence they had come three days prior. Fighting Joe Hooker's lack of aggressiveness allowed the Confederate commander to again get away with dividing his army.

On May 3 and 4, fighting raged around the Salem church between Fredericksburg and Chancellorsville. For the first time in the battle, Lee was able to amass on this part of the field slightly more men than the Federals.

After a final Confederate assault on the evening of the fourth, the Union troops forming the southern jaw of the now-shattered vise withdrew back across the Rappahannock to safety.

Ever the aggressor, Lee turned his troops around and headed off to do battle with the other contingent of Union soldiers to his rear. There would be no further fighting at Chancellorsville, however. During the night, Hooker gave the order for all his remaining troops to retreat back to the other side of the river.

Lee's audacious response had turned Hooker's "perfect" plan into a shocking disaster.

From Stone Wall to Foot Cavalry
JACKSON'S VALLEY CAMPAIGN, 1862

Robert E. Lee's victory at Chancellorsville has been hailed as one of the greatest military victories in history. But Lee also suffered his greatest loss there.

Returning in darkness from reconnoitering in front of his lines, Stonewall Jackson was accidentally shot by his own troops. Just hours after routing Union General Joe Hooker's right flank, Jackson was on his way to the rear, where he would succumb to his wounds.

Lee and Jackson were the greatest military pairing in history. The brilliant, aristocratic Lee would sketch out a strategy and the rumpled, energetic Jackson would turn that strategy into battlefield tactics—and into victories.

The Lee–Jackson "team" made its debut in the spring of 1862, twelve months before Chancellorsville. Lee was serving as military adviser to Confederate President Jefferson Davis and Jackson was commanding a small force in Virginia's Shenandoah Valley.

In their first collaboration they demonstrated how a bold response can overcome an enemy's greater strength and derail the opponent's strategic plan.

Union General George McClellan was advancing up the Virginia peninsula toward Richmond with 100,000 men, far outnumbering the Confederate defenders, as described in Lesson One.

Claiming he needed even more soldiers to assure success, McClellan requisitioned another 50,000 Federal troops, who had been assigned to defend Washington and environs, under the command of Major General Nathaniel P. Banks.

Robert E. Lee had to quickly devise a plan to keep those additional Union troops from joining the assault on the Rebel capital, or all would be lost. The general he chose to carry out this strategy was the hero of First Manassas (Bull Run), Thomas "Stonewall" Jackson.

Lee sketched out his plan in a message to Jackson. Stonewall's assignment was to threaten Washington and thereby force Lincoln to retain Banks' units for the defense of the Federal capital.

"Whatever movement you make against Banks, do it speedily," Lee's message instructed, "and if successful drive him back toward the Potomac and create the impression, as far as practicable, that you intend to threaten that line."

That was all the strategic direction Stonewall required. With a force that never exceeded 18,000 men, Jackson kept 60,000 Union troops occupied and away from Richmond. During a crucial thirty-day period in May and June of 1862, Jackson's men played hide and seek with Union forces by marching 350 miles—up and down the Shenandoah Valley five times. They fought four major battles, winning them all, kept three enemy armies divided and tied down, and at the last moment were able to slip off to throw their weight into the battle on the peninsula.

Jackson's success is a measurable example of the fruits of employing a bold counter-strategy to overcome an enemy's smart plan. The Union troops McClellan had sought from Washington as essential to his effort to capture Richmond never arrived. They were kept far away, chasing or guarding against the elusive Jackson.

In *Fields of Battle* John Keagan, perhaps the greatest military historian of our time, described Jackson's audacious strategy: "To run his soldiers as harshly as he ran himself, to march them so fast from strategic point to point that they earned the name 'foot cavalry,' to live off the land, to drub Union forces wherever found, but above all, to so 'mystify and mislead' that the enemy always fought divided and never succeeded in uniting against him."

• • •

The Shenandoah Valley was the breadbasket of Virginia. Running northeast to southwest, from Harpers Ferry in the north down to Staunton, the valley opened on the back door to Washington and was permeated by mountain passes through which an army could slip into the northern Virginia countryside to threaten the Union capital.

The valley of the Shenandoah River is approximately 120 miles long, defined by the Blue Ridge Mountains on the east and the Allegheny Mountains on the west. About one third of the way down the valley, the river splits around the forty-mile-long Massanutten Mountain.

This geography, combined with Jackson's hard-driving generalship, confounded the Union command. Keagan describes Jackson's Valley Campaign as "an essay in the pure use of terrain for which there are few parallels in military history." Simply put, Jackson did what "couldn't be done." By moving farther and faster than infantry was supposed to be capable of doing, he seized the strategic initiative despite being overwhelmingly outnumbered.

Jackson's tactics were summed up in a message to one of his officers toward the end of the Valley Campaign: "Always mystify, mislead and surprise the enemy, if possible. And when you strike and overcome him, never let up in pursuit so long as your men have the strength to follow . . . Such tactics will win every time, and a small army may thus destroy a large one in detail, and repeated victory will make it invincible."

In March 1862, Stonewall Jackson suffered the only battlefield defeat of his career, at Kernstown, toward the northern end of the valley. That the battle even occurred was a measure of Jackson's audacity. He saw General Banks' troops withdrawing northward toward Washington, and rather than let them get away to join McClellan's army at Richmond, Jackson attacked even though he was outnumbered two to one.

Jackson's tactical defeat at the Battle of Kernstown, however, turned out to be a strategic victory. Banks, unable to conceive that an inferior Confederate force would attack a superior Union force, concluded that Jackson's Rebel army must be a greater threat to Washington than previously imagined. With the consent of Lincoln and McClellan, Banks abandoned his plan to join the Union advance on Richmond.

In addition, Lincoln reinforced the garrison around Washington with another 10,000 troops who had been headed for duty in the peninsula.

Kernstown proved the value of tactical audacity. The Confederate defense of Richmond was tremendously aided by Stonewall's offensive in the Shenandoah Valley.

Moving southward, Jackson lured the Union troops deeper into the valley. By early May, Banks had pursued Jackson almost the entire length of the valley. Union Major General John Frémont, commanding in what today is West Virginia, sent troops from the west to join Banks in an effort to crush the pesky Confederate.

Jackson misled his opponents by marching his troops east, away from the Union forces and out of the valley. Having created the impression that he was on the way to reinforce Richmond, Jackson then loaded his men onto trains and headed back into the valley. Unloading at Staunton, he marched further west, defeated Frémont's troops at the Battle of McDowell on May 8, and pursued them into western Virginia.

Believing that Jackson was tied down in the far southern end of the valley, Lincoln began to feel more secure about the capital. He ordered Union troops guarding Washington to reinforce McClellan's advance on Richmond. Even some of Banks' men in the valley were ordered to pull back to Washington in preparation for transfer to the peninsula.

Having defeated Frémont's force from the west, Jackson made

a surprise move, cut through the only pass in the Massanutten Mountain, marched sixty miles in three days, and moved up the east side of the Shenandoah Valley. On May 23, with the majority of the Union forces on the west side of the valley, Jackson fell upon and devastated the Union garrison at Front Royal.

Union General Banks, fearing that Jackson would get between him and Washington, withdrew up the valley to Winchester. Jackson anticipated Banks' move, however, and beat him to Winchester, defeating the Union troops there on May 25.

The Confederates captured so many Union supplies in the rout that they began calling the opposing general "Commissary Banks."

Stonewall drove Banks north, back toward the Potomac. This push north once again threatened Washington. For the second time, Lincoln rescinded the transfer of Union troops to the peninsula.

Lincoln himself now envisioned a strategy to trap Jackson in the north end of the valley and punish him for his audacity.

From the west, General Frémont moved his forces eastward. From the east, came other Federal forces. The units would converge south of Jackson's position, cutting off his withdrawal and allowing the Federal forces to crush his army.

But the ever-daring Jackson, marching his troops fifty miles in two days, eluded the trap.

Next, the Federal commanders decided to send their troops down both sides of the valley to foil Jackson's elusive maneuvers.

"We'll stop his sliding back and forth," Banks promised.

Again, the Federals underestimated Stonewall. On June 8, Confederate troops defeated Frémont's western column at Cross Keys. On June 9, the Confederates defeated the eastern column at Port Republic. The Union forces retreated northward, again.

But instead of pursing them, this time Jackson slipped away through a gap in the Blue Ridge Mountains. Having successfully fulfilled Lee's strategy to keep Union reinforcements from reaching Richmond, Jackson now directly joined the fight to save the Confederate capital.

Seventeen days after their last battle in the Shenandoah Valley, Jackson's men attacked McClellan outside of Richmond, beginning the campaign which drove Union troops from the gates of the Southern capital.

Jackson's audacious implementation of Lee's strategy had worked miracles. The mind games with Lincoln and the Union forces had succeeded in preventing reinforcements from participating in the assault on Richmond, while Jackson's men not only accomplished their goal but were also able to play a crucial role in pushing McClellan back down the peninsula.

Audacity Trumps Audacity
EARLY'S ATTACK ON WASHINGTON

In the summer of 1864, Robert E. Lee needed a bold move to shift the tide of the war, which was running in the Union's favor. With Stonewall Jackson in his grave, Lee turned to Lieutenant General Jubal Early to lead a bold attack on Washington, D.C. By itself, Early's raid is a wonderful example of leadership audacity. The example becomes even more poignant, however, because of the boldness of the self-appointed Union leader who determined its outcome.

At the very time when Ulysses S. Grant was increasing Union pressure on the Confederate capital, Robert E. Lee ordered Jubal Early to pull 14,000 men out of Richmond's defenses and march north.

Grant had massed virtually the entire Army of the Potomac to take the Confederate capital. The thought of a mere 14,000 Rebels capturing the Union capital must have seemed beyond audacious, verging on the preposterous.

It was, however, worth the try, given the opening created

when Grant stripped Washington of its defenders in order to strengthen his forces besieging Richmond. Fewer than 10,000 men in blue remained to garrison the thirty-seven miles of fortifications ringing the Federal capital. Most of these troops were the Veteran Reserve Corps—men who, because of wounds or sickness, were judged unfit for the front line.

If Early could fall upon Washington before Grant could send reinforcements, he would capture not only the seat of government, its Treasury, and principal supply depot but also send shock waves through the war-weary North as it headed into a presidential election. Capturing Washington might even persuade France and Britain to finally intervene on behalf of the Confederates. Achieving such deliverance fell to forty-seven-year-old Jubal Early. Like so many other leaders in the war, Early was a product of West Point who dropped out of the military to pursue a civilian career. When war came, he gave up his law practice in southwest Virginia for a colonel's commission in the Confederate army. Steadily, "Jube" Early rose in responsibility until, by the summer of 1864, he was a lieutenant general, commanding the II Corps and reporting directly to Lee.

Profane, with a plug of tobacco constantly stuck in his jaw, Early had not always been brilliant on the battlefield—but his leadership had demonstrated the kind of boldness and audacity now required of him.

On June 13, 1864, Early's men left Richmond, bound for the north. Their pathway would be the Shenandoah Valley. First, however, they had to deal with a Federal force blocking their way at the southern end of the valley.

On June 18, Early's four divisions joined another Rebel division at Lynchburg, Virginia, commanded by Major General John C. Breckinridge (the former U.S. Vice President who had been defeated by Lincoln for the presidency in 1860). The Confederates, although outnumbered, not only repulsed a Federal attack but also drove the Bluecoats from the valley.

The march north toward Washington resumed.

By the first week in July, Early's army had crossed the Potomac into Maryland. Passing through Sharpsburg, site of the Battle of Antietam two years previously, Early used the same passes through the Maryland mountains that Union General George McClellan had used on his way from Washington to confront the Rebels at Antietam. This time, however, the marchers in the passes wore butternut gray and were advancing *toward* Washington.

For the first time, the Union high command perceived the threat to the Federal capital. Grant, realizing that Early was not still in front of him outside Richmond, rushed a corps of the Army of the Potomac from Richmond by boat to reinforce Washington. Lincoln asked Northern governors to send short-term draftees to the capital's defense.

But with Early through the Maryland mountains, there was no Union force between his Confederates and the Federal capital. Until the reinforcements arrived from Grant, the only substantial Union forces even in proximity of Washington were a ragtag collection of Maryland Home Militia and a few ninety-day volunteers charged with defending Baltimore. Commanding the Baltimore defenders was Major General Lew Wallace, exiled to that administrative backwater after his abysmal performance at the Battle of Shiloh, where he marched his men in every direction except into battle.

Wallace saw what had to be done, and saw a chance for redemption. His plan, however, required not one, but two audacious decisions.

First he would expose Baltimore—his appointed responsibility—by moving his men between Early and Washington. If he was wrong and Early was really after Baltimore and the Point Lookout prisoner of war camp nearby, the city Wallace was ordered to protect would be defenseless.

Wallace's second audacious decision was to act without telling his superiors, out of fear they were still so down on him for Shiloh that they would countermand his decision.

After the war, Wallace wrote the immensely popular *Ben-Hur.* In the early days of July 1864, he took action worthy of the fictional hero of his epic.

It was a battle against time. Jubal Early was racing to reach Washington before Grant's reinforcements arrived. Lew Wallace's job was to slow down the Rebels.

Wallace gathered up whomever he could find—a sparse force of about 3,000 men—and moved them to a defensive position along the Monocacy River, a tributary of the Potomac about thirty miles in front of Washington.

On the day before Early reached his position, 3,000 veterans reinforced Wallace, the first of Grant's men from Richmond. The reinforcements landed at Baltimore and were proceeding by rail to Harpers Ferry when they were intercepted by Wallace and pressed into the Union line at the Monocacy.

When Early and his Confederate soldiers arrived, they found the three bridges spanning the stream were well covered by Wallace's men (who, even after reinforcement, were still outnumbered by better than two to one). The Rebels set out to look for another crossing further downriver to flank the Federals. Wallace had anticipated such a move, however, and had placed his best troops, Grant's veterans, on that flank.

First the Bluecoats repulsed a dismounted Confederate cavalry advance. Then the Rebel infantry made it across the river and attacked. It was a long afternoon for Wallace's men, but they held their position. Finally, however, the Rebel infantry's third assault broke the left end of the Union line and another Early division prevailed on the right flank.

Wallace and his men withdrew toward Baltimore, having lost almost 1,900 soldiers to Early's 700. But because Wallace's men had stood astride the path to Washington and clung to that position for a full day, Early lost more than men—he lost time.

The next day, Early pressed on, ignoring the ninety-degree-plus heat and humidity. By the end of the day, the Confederates had progressed about half the distance to Washington. One more day's marching would put them at their objective.

The fighting and forced marching, however, had taken its toll on Early's troops. While their general—who had ridden ahead of the main body of troops—was inspecting the Union defenses through binoculars, his men and their animals were falling to heat prostration and exhaustion.

Early was in front of Fort Stevens, one of the ring of defensive earthen works surrounding the capital.

"The works were but feebly manned," Early would write later. But Early was feebly manned himself and could not muster sufficient troops for an immediate attack. As he waited for the main body of his troops to appear, Early saw through his field glasses a cloud of dust approaching the fort from the south—Grant's reinforcements.

That night—July 11, 1864—Jubal Early held a council of war with his division commanders. They would attack the next day, he decided. They had come too far to turn back now.

During the night, however, word reached Early that he was facing not one but two corps of Union veterans. The Confederate attack was canceled to await what daylight would reveal.

"As soon as it was light enough to see, I rode to the front and saw the parapet lined with troops," Early wrote. The die was cast. There would be no attack on the Federal capital. The Rebels would remain in position facing Fort Stevens that day and withdraw that night, hoping to catch the jump on the Federals for a wild dash back across the Potomac to Confederate territory.

Despite failing to achieve its goal, Jubal Early's audacious raid on Washington had produced some positive results—lessening by two corps the Union pressure on Richmond and demonstrating to the Northern electorate that the war was far from over and that they were far from immune.

It was General Wallace's bold action, however, that prevented Early's success. Wallace's decision to lead 3,000 ragtags against a rumored 30,000 man Rebel force saved the day.

The Early advance on Washington produced a unique historical footnote. Among those on the parapet at Fort Stevens on July 12 was President Abraham Lincoln, stovepipe hat and all. As Confederate snipers and sharpshooters popped away, Lincoln curiously surveyed the field.

When a man standing close to the President was hit, Captain Oliver Wendell Holmes roared at Lincoln, "Get down, you damn fool, before you get shot!"

Lincoln, thus, became the only sitting President to come under enemy fire in battle. Holmes, wounded three times during the war, went on to become one of America's greatest jurists as Chief Justice of the United States Supreme Court.

Years later, when a member of Early's staff, Henry Kyd Douglas, wrote of his war experiences, he recounted Early's words on the last day on the outskirts of Washington, "Major, we haven't taken Washington, but we've scared Abe Lincoln like hell!"

The Plan to Demolish CNN
TED TURNER VERSUS ABC/GROUP W

Ted Turner is the Stonewall Jackson of today's business world— and he relishes the role.

In the early years of Turner Broadcasting, as president of the National Cable Television Association, I'd sit in Turner's office while he brandished a Confederate battle sword over his head. He was in the midst of a war, Turner would declare, a life or death struggle equal to the great conflicts of history.

"Everything I do is war," he once said. "It's a war between the forces of good and evil, hatred and stupidity, greed and material-ism versus the forces of light."

Turner wasn't exaggerating by much—he was rewriting the way people around the world received information, and for him it was a life-or-death conflict. Starting with a billboard company and a last-in-the-market Atlanta UHF television station, Turner had used the new phenomenon of cable television to build a media company that threatened the entrenched media powers.

And the networks didn't like it. Earlier they said it couldn't be done. But Turner had done it. At a time when the major televi-sion networks focused their news activities on thirty-minute evening news shows, Ted Turner had built a twenty-four-hour all-news television network from scratch. And advertisers and subscribers were paying for it!

"Does Ted Turner know something that the networks don't?" asked the *New York Times*.

The broadcast television networks finally woke up to the threat Turner represented to their hegemony. The ABC Televi-sion Network led the charge, supported by Westinghouse Corpo-ration's broadcast division, Group W.

Together they arrayed their vast resources to teach the Philis-tine Turner a lesson by launching their own twenty-four-hour television news service. It was formidable competition for the struggling CNN, just sixteen months old and still losing money by the bucketful.

ABC was a powerhouse television network whose news divi-sion was headed by Roone Arledge, the man who had made the network number one in sports. Westinghouse Corporation's Group W Broadcasting owned the largest group of radio and television stations in the country and, most important, one of the largest chains of cable systems.

ABC intended to provide the network resources and Group W the cable outlets for the assault on Turner and CNN. Together they were prepared to spend $40 to $60 million to launch two Satellite News Channel (SNC) services. The first to launch would be a headline news service patterned after Group W's successful news radio format, with its highly promoted motto, "Give us eighteen minutes and we'll give you the world." The second service would be an in-depth news channel very similar to CNN.

ABC/Group W had the news-gathering resources, years of experience, guaranteed outlets, and bottomless corporate pockets to send Turner back to his billboard business.

A few months after the SNC announcement, a research study commissioned by Compton Advertising expressed the common wisdom: "Turner will enjoy a short-term advantage, [but] the ABC-Westinghouse venture will dominate by 1990."

The Compton report forecast that ultimately "a merger or outright sale will be necessary for Turner to keep a competitive position."

In its opening salvo against Turner, ABC and Westinghouse went for the jugular — SNC would be transmitted *free* to cable system operators. By contrast, Turner was charging cable systems for CNN and supporting his financially precarious house of cards with those revenues.

By subsidizing SNC, the deep-pocketed corporate parents were able to create a double-whammy—cutting costs for cable system operators while making sure that Turner earned less money.

Ted Turner's Stonewall-like response to this threat was to attack.

He summoned his lieutenants and announced that CNN would start its own headline news channel and would have it operational before SNC. Like Jackson, who never held a council of war to ask his generals what they thought, the meeting Turner called was to issue orders, not solicit opinions. His decision had been made; it was now up to everyone to implement that decision.

Turner's chief financial officer argued that establishing the new headline service would bankrupt the company. Turner's response: *Attack!*

The ad sales team warned that the already-fragile market for their product would fragment. *Attack!* Turner directed them.

The affiliate relations staff, whose job it was to persuade cable systems to carry CNN, complained that it was hard enough to sell them one channel of news, now they would have to convince cable operators to pay for two channels. *Attack!* Turner commanded.

His aides were right to raise concerns about Turner's decision to start a second all-news channel. His undercapitalized and understaffed CNN was already stretched thin fulfilling the promise of around-the-clock news. Now, like Lee at Chancellorsville, Turner was proposing to split his embattled forces for the new battle with ABC/Westinghouse.

"Ted's happy," CNN president Reese Schoenfeld is reported to have said as he left the meeting. "We're at war again."

Two weeks after the SNC announcement, Turner appeared at a cable industry meeting in Boston to announce CNN2, "a compact, hard-news service catering to viewers who want a quicker, more concise summary of the day's events."

The battle was joined.

And almost immediately Roone Arledge, the president of ABC News, made a senseless tactical error.

"Our first priority remains our network news operation," Arledge unthinkingly declared, trying to reassure his broadcast affiliates. "Our facilities will just supply extra footage for the cable service that won't be in competition with broadcast news . . . If Barbara Walters were to interview the Ayatollah Khomeini, obviously we would consider that an exclusive for 'ABC World News Tonight.' "

Never expose your flank like that to Ted Turner.

Turner jumped on Arledge's statement as proof that SNC

would offer cable operators and subscribers only the cast-offs of network news. At the Boston cable meeting, Turner thundered, "Anybody who goes with them is going with a second-rate, horseshit operation!"

And that was just the first of a series of masterful attacks. A frontal assault was impossible against the massed firepower of ABC and Westinghouse. So Turner fought smaller skirmishes of his own choosing, keeping the opposition at bay, appearing to be everywhere at once, acting like Jackson in the valley.

Like Jackson, Turner set marching orders that, to others, seemed unachievable. He decreed that CNN2 would launch before SNC, despite the fact that SNC had a head start in planning its headline service. Turner expected his troops to launch their version in just four months, on December 31, 1981.

Turner identified and fell upon a strategic weakness of his opposition. SNC planned to use a yet-to-be-launched satellite, Westar-4, to deliver its programming to cable systems. Most cable systems weren't yet equipped with antennas to receive the Westar-4 satellite.

Turner would gain a great advantage if CNN2 was transmitted by the principal cable delivery satellite, Satcom-1, which cable systems were already equipped to receive. The problem was that capacity on that satellite was sold out.

There was one possibility, however—a vacant transponder owned by Warner Communications on Satcom-1. Turner approached Warner and its cable partner, American Express, with a deal they couldn't refuse—put CNN2 on the satellite and, in return, Turner would give Warner-Amex the exclusive right to sell all the advertising time (and receive the sales commissions) on CNN and CNN2 for the next two years.

It was a huge price for Turner to pay. But it would give CNN2 a significant leg up in the battle with his new and powerful competitor. While SNC would have to convince cable operators to invest in new satellite-receiving equipment and then wait for its installation, CNN2 could offer immediate delivery with no additional capital expense.

Turner's next audacious tactic was to carry the battle to his enemy's home territory. He offered CNN2 as a service to broadcast television stations. If the broadcast networks were going to compete on his cable turf, he decided he'd damn well compete on their broadcast turf. Within a year, more than 100 local TV stations had signed up for CNN2. Not only would these stations carry CNN2's news items, but they also gave Turner permission to rebroadcast their news coverage, thus expanding CNN's news-gathering capability at virtually no cost.

ABC/Westinghouse did not sit still. Using their financial strength, the two network powerhouses announced they would not just provide SNC free to cable operators, they would actually *pay* cable operators fifty cents per subscriber per year to carry SNC.

"Westinghouse and ABC would certainly seem to have the finances to outgun Turner if they have a mind to," *Broadcasting* magazine observed.

CNN2 launched, as Turner had ordained, on December 31, 1981, with fewer than 1 million homes subscribing. SNC launched six months later, on June 21, 1982, with 2.6 million homes.

Now the war was really on!

In that war, Ted Turner was the personification of Stonewall Jackson's admonition to mystify, mislead, and never let up. You never knew what Turner would do—or say—next. But you could be sure he wouldn't sit still or remain quiet.

As CNN president Reese Schoenfeld observed, "Ted's reaction to competition is to go on the offensive. It's the only way he knows to respond. He feeds on risk, and his appetite is insatiable."

Turner appealed to the loyalty of cable operators, reminding them that in the days when ABC and the other broadcasters had been trying to shut down the fledgling medium, he had been their champion.

"I was cable before cable was cool" was his advertising campaign.

At the same time, Turner attacked SNC's parents, joining an ongoing national assault against the quality of network television programming.

"What those networks are doing is making Hitler Youth out of the American people," Turner roared. "They ought to be tried for treason; they're the worst enemies America's ever had."

If the broadcast networks would go against his lifeblood, he'd go against theirs, telling a committee of the House of Representatives, "The network's own television licenses should be revoked immediately and given to responsible citizens who will do good."

Turner's final assault came in the courts. He would sue SNC, ABC, and Westinghouse. When his attorney counseled the absence of grounds for an effective suit, Turner reportedly replied, "Well, dammit, find one!"

The result was an antitrust case against SNC and Group W charging collusion to keep CNN's products off the Westinghouse-owned cable systems.

The suit did two things: forced ABC and Westinghouse to pour even more money into their fledgling cable news project and uncovered in the discovery process documents allegedly supporting Turner's contention. Those documents, in a trial, might threaten the very ability of ABC and Group W to hold their broadcast licenses.

For almost two years, ABC and Westinghouse experienced what it was like to be at war with Ted Turner. Their new, seemingly brilliant undertaking had cost far more than they'd planned. Their core broadcasting activities were under siege. And now the legal process seemed to be opening up another vulnerability.

The Westinghouse board decided to seek a truce. One day in

late 1983, I received a call from a Group W executive inquiring how I thought the cable operators I represented would react if SNC sought to settle the war and asking who might be the appropriate mediator to help the parties negotiate a peace.

The end of the war was in sight. A negotiating committee was established with one of cable's true pioneers, Bill Daniels, as the third-party mediator. On October 12, in a retreat as abject as General Hooker's from Chancellorsville, ABC and Westinghouse sold SNC to Ted Turner for $25 million. Typically, he had to scramble to borrow the money.

Two weeks later, an SNC anchorman signed off, "That's it for now. In fact, that's it, period. And now, Ted buddy, it's in your hands!"

Marching Orders

Boldness and audacity can often trump a perfect plan and make up for inferior resources.

Stonewall Jackson did what others assumed could not be done and, thus, prevailed. Jackson's admonition to "always mystify, mislead, and surprise" really meant make your opponent respond to you.

Ted Turner instinctively knew his survival depended on the fact that he never lose the offensive. One way of keeping his opponent off guard was to always do the unpredictable.

Like Stonewall Jackson, Turner's tactics brought him ultimate victory and, for Turner, a position as one of the world's media giants.

Lesson Six

Information Is Only Critical If It Is Used Properly

Use it or lose it

"Warfare is 90 percent information," counseled Napoleon. Time has not dulled that maxim. Its mere possession, however, means little. The outcomes of struggles are determined by what is *done with* the information.

The events leading up to the Battle of Antietam (Sharpsburg) in 1862 were driven by the use of information. What happened during those days shaped the battle's outcome—the bloodiest day in American history.

The leaders of the two armies, the Union's George McClellan and the Confederacy's Robert E. Lee, could not have been more different in their use of the information in their possession.

Lee, an information scavenger, used mere shards of intelligence to overcome numerical and tactical inferiority. McClellan squandered a mother lode of information that fell into his lap.

Antietam demonstrated that unless information is put to use in a timely manner it is of little value.

Information Used and Information Squandered
THE CAMPAIGNS OF 1862

As Ulysses S. Grant rode to the site of the Rebel counterattack at Fort Donelson in 1862, as related in Lesson Two, he noticed that Rebel prisoners being led to the rear had full haversacks. Ordering one of the prisoners brought to him, he opened the pack to discover food for a multi-day march.

Fletcher Pratt's *Ordeal by Fire* records Grant saying, "These men are trying to escape. They have rations for a long march, not a fight. All the strength must be on this side. Tell General Smith to attack the fort on his front at once."

Based on a seemingly small observation, Grant quickly launched an offensive. The attack prevailed precisely for the reason Grant had foreseen—the Rebels were making a break for it, weakening their defenses. Fort Donelson surrendered to Grant that night.

Six months later, in Virginia, Confederate General Robert E. Lee's army needed a similar scrap of information to gauge the intentions of Union Major General George B. McClellan.

Having been driven from the gates of Richmond, the Union army was holed up in secure positions on the Virginia peninsula. Would they move from those positions toward Richmond again, or back north?

Rebel spies in Washington informed Lee that McClellan's men would be returning to Washington. Lee quickly acted on the information. Its capital no longer in danger, soon the Confederate army was repositioned in northern Virginia.

The result (see Lesson One) was the Second Battle of Manassas (Bull Run). The speed with which Lee reacted to the spies' intelligence meant that virtually his entire army reached Manassas well ahead of the Union troops coming from the peninsula. It was the decisive factor in the battle and brought Lee another victory.

After the battle at Manassas, Lee headed north. It was time to take the fight to the farms and villages of the enemy. By early September, the Rebel army was marching along the roads of the Northern state of Maryland.

The invasion of Maryland would produce the war's greatest examples of the use of information. One general would squander a treasure trove that fell into his lap. The other general would use mere scraps of information brilliantly to his advantage.

Lee's plan was to cross into Pennsylvania, capture the state capital of Harrisburg, and destroy its strategic bridge across the Susquehanna River. Having destroyed other strategic points on his march, destruction of the Harrisburg bridge would force Union transportation between the battlefields of the east and west to detour via less direct routes through northern Pennsylvania, southern New York, and the Great Lakes.

After taking Harrisburg, Lee expected to "turn my attention to Philadelphia, Baltimore or Washington, as may seem best for our interests."

In order to accomplish this grand plan, the Confederates had to open a new line of communication and supply between Lee's advancing army and the Rebel bases below the Mason-Dixon line. The Shenandoah Valley provided the perfect avenue. First, however, the Federal outposts at the north end of the valley, at Martinsburg and Harpers Ferry, had to be neutralized.

On September 9, despite the fact that he was being pursued by a larger Federal force under McClellan, Lee ordered his command split. The bulk of the Confederate troops were sent to eliminate the Union garrisons atop the Shenandoah Valley, while Lee proceeded north with only about one third of his army.

Lee's daring plan was written up as Special Orders No. 191. Copies were made for distribution by courier to his division commanders. Because one of those commanders, Major General D. H. Hill, enjoyed a good smoke, someone at headquarters thoughtfully included in his dispatch envelope three cigars, wrapped in a copy of Special Orders No. 191.

The plan was to take effect the following morning. Stonewall Jackson would lead his troops back across the Potomac into Virginia to dispose of the Martinsburg post and then move on Harpers Ferry from the west. Two other columns would march to encircle the other sides of Harpers Ferry.

Once again, Lee had violated one of the immutable military maxims—he had split his army in the face of a superior force. What's more, he had broken his army into four parts, some separated from the rest by the Potomac River.

But Lee reckoned the risk was small.

"General McClellan is an able general but a very cautious one," the Confederate commander opined. By the time his opponent got around to taking action, Lee concluded, the divided Southern forces would have secured the mouth of the Shenandoah and would have reunited in Maryland.

On September 13, four days after Special Orders No. 191 was drafted, a company of Union infantry set up its camp outside of Frederick, Maryland. A corporal noticed a bulky envelope lying in the grass. Inside were three cigars—a glorious discovery for any man suffering the deprivations of the field.

Wrapped around the stogies was an even more valuable discovery: a sheet of paper headed, "Hd Qrs Army of Northern Va Sept 9th 1862." It was a copy of Lee's Special Orders No. 191, intended for General Hill, but somehow gone terribly astray.

Soon General McClellan had in his hands the fondest dream of any commander—the detailed plan of his opponent. There, in black and white, was Lee's own description of his objective, the disposition of his troops, their routes of travel, and their timetable for battle.

When an aide brought the document to McClellan, the general was meeting with a group of local citizens. After reading the miraculous find, he threw up his hands and exclaimed, "Now I know what to do!" The locals were quickly ushered out.

For days McClellan had been sifting through reports of Lee's maneuvers, trying to divine his intentions. After reading the orders, he knew everything about Lee's plans. Moreover, he perceived how vulnerable Lee's divided forces were to attack.

McClellan immediately sent a telegram to President Lincoln.

"I have the whole rebel force in front of me, but am confident, and no time shall be lost," the Union commander wrote. "I think Lee has made a gross mistake, and that he will be severely punished for it . . . I have all the plans of the rebels, and will catch them in their own trap if my men are equal to the emergency."

Waving the misplaced Confederate plans, McClellan boasted to Brigadier General John Gibbon, "Here is a paper with which if I cannot whip Bobby Lee, I will be willing to go home."

In actuality, the Rebel position was even more vulnerable than Special Orders No. 191 portrayed. After issuing the Orders, Lee received an (incorrect) report of a Federal column moving down from Pennsylvania and split off part of his forces yet again to intercept it.

As a result, the Confederate force confronting McClellan's almost 90,000 men in the Maryland countryside consisted of a single Confederate division. All the rest of the Rebels were around Harpers Ferry, marching with Lee to meet the phantom threat from Pennsylvania, or still on the Virginia side of the Potomac.

Defeating Lee's army should have been a walk in the park for

George McClellan. After all, he had Lee's plans, and the nine outnumbered Confederate divisions were now split into five parts, widely separated.

"My general idea is to cut the enemy in two & beat him in detail," McClellan told one of his generals. He began to savor the forthcoming victory, comparing the situation (and himself) to Napoleon's defeat of an overextended Austrian army at Castiglione in 1796.

"Tomorrow we will pitch into [Lee's] center and if you people will only do two good, hard days' marching, I will put Lee in a position he will find it hard to get out of," the self-styled Napoleon told a subordinate.

Tomorrow? Why would McClellan wait overnight before attacking his vulnerable enemy?

Lee's Lost Orders had reached the Federal general before noon on September 13. There still remained a good seven hours of daylight. The gaps in South Mountain through which the Federal force would have to pass to catch Lee's troops could be reached before dark.

Possessing priceless information, McClellan failed to make timely use of his coup.

Any commander worth his stars would have put his army in motion immediately. But McClellan chose to wait. The first Union troops finally began their march to engage the Rebel soldiers a full eighteen hours after McClellan received Lee's Lost Orders.

Historians still debate whether Robert E. Lee knew that George McClellan had obtained a copy of his battle plans. Confederate procedures required that the envelopes in which Special Orders No. 191 were delivered to Lee's commanders were to be returned to headquarters, signed by the recipient, as proof of receipt. No contemporary record or report references that General Hill's envelope was missing.

It is known that a Southern sympathizer, who was among the Maryland townspeople meeting with McClellan shortly after he received the Lost Orders, heard the Union general exclaim, "Now I know what to do!"

The Southern sympathizer promptly reported this to Lee's cavalry commander, General J. E. B. Stuart, who told Lee. Therefore, the Southern commander knew about McClellan's exultation, but probably did not know that coming into possession of the Lost Orders had occasioned it.

After the war, Lee suggested that he knew a copy of his Orders had been lost and discovered by the Federals. But, in all likelihood, that was hindsight. Lee probably did not learn that McClellan had obtained a copy of the Lost Orders until months later when the press reported on the Union commander's testimony before Congress, in which he revealed the discovery.

Regardless of whether he knew that his Orders had been found by the Federals, Lee did receive one bit of intelligence while his forces were maneuvering through Maryland. Stuart reported that some Union troops were on the move, although he didn't know where they were going or why. (As it turned out, this particular deployment was not related to the Lost Orders.)

Lee was not one to sit on even such a slim and unsubstantial piece of information. As soon as he learned that Union soldiers were moving "more rapidly than was convenient," as he described the situation to President Davis a few days later, Lee reacted.

On the morning of September 14—the day McClellan finally began his offensive against the Rebels in response to the disclosures in the Lost Orders—Lee acted on the report of Union troop movements by ordering his divisions near the Pennsylvania border to retrace their steps and reinforce the lone division confronting the Federals.

Between the Union troops and the dispersed Rebels was a spur of the Blue Ridge Mountains called South Mountain. The Confederate stand against the Federal advance was made at the passes of South Mountain.

It was a stand where every minute counted. At first, the vastly outnumbered Rebel defenders were forced to fight Indian-style from behind walls and trees. But Lee's decision to react quickly to Stuart's intelligence about Federal troop movements saved the day. The fresh Confederate soldiers recalled from the Pennsylvania border turned the tide despite the two to one Federal superiority on the field.

McClellan's slow reaction upon discovery of the vital information in the Lost Orders had given Lee the gift of twenty-four hours to prepare for the battle. Had the Union commander moved the day before, when he first obtained the intelligence about the dispersed Confederate troop dispositions, Rebel reinforcements never would have reached the South Mountain passes in time to stop the Union advance.

And holding off the larger Union army at the mountain passes had bought Lee another day to save his army. By the evening of the Battle of South Mountain (September 14), the Confederate general sent a message to his dispersed command that he was abandoning his position and falling back toward the Potomac. He urged his subordinates to do likewise.

On the fifteenth, Lee withdrew from South Mountain and regrouped about eight miles away along Antietam Creek, outside Sharpsburg, Maryland.

Amazingly, McClellan did not exploit his advantage by pursuing the Rebels until the next day, September 16. Another gift of time to Lee from a commander who was frittering away his great intelligence coup.

As Lee pulled back to Antietam, one of his dispersed units under Stonewall Jackson captured Harpers Ferry, having earlier taken Martinsburg. Successfully completing his assignment,

Jackson immediately set out to rejoin Lee's force at Sharpsburg. When he got there, the divided Confederate forces would be reunited, save for one unit.

The Union side would lose the advantage of the Lost Orders if the Confederate troops were permitted to reconcentrate.

September 16 was George McClellan's fourth and final opportunity to use his intelligence windfall. Until Jackson arrived with his soldiers, Lee sat exposed outside of Sharpsburg with only 15,000 men facing McClellan's 90,000 Union troops. But the Union general who fancied himself a "Young Napoleon" certainly didn't act like Napoleon. The hesitant McClellan did not attack Lee on the sixteenth. He waited still another day before launching his assault, initiating the Battle of Antietam described in Lesson One. McClellan had sat on his priceless information far too long. By the time he attacked, Jackson's troops had begun to arrive, continuing to come in throughout the battle, steadily strengthening the Confederate forces.

At a time when a few hours could have changed the outcome at South Mountain and later at Antietam, George McClellan gave Robert E. Lee the invaluable gift of time by failing to make use of the information he had.

Lee described the Lost Orders as a "great calamity" which "changed the character of the campaign." It enabled McClellan, Lee said, "to discover my whereabouts . . . and caused him so to act as to force a battle on me before I was ready for it."

Historian Stephen Sears wrote in *The Landscape Turned Red,* "It was said that in later years, of all his battles, General Lee took the most pride in Sharpsburg. When it became clear how destructive the loss of Order 191 was to his plan of campaign, he felt that never before or after did his army face greater odds."

Lee's timely use of a few scraps of information reversed those odds. While McClellan squandered a banquet of information that had been delivered to him on a silver platter, Lee, with only morsels of data, maneuvered his forces shrewdly and with vigor, avoiding what almost certainly would have been a disaster.

McClellan's September 13 boast, "Here is a paper with which if I cannot whip Bobby Lee, I will be willing to go home," proved prescient. Shortly after the Battle of Antietam, Lincoln sacked him.

The Information Business
IT'S THE INFORMATION BEHIND THE BUSINESS

Federal Express is in the delivery business; Dell Computer is in the computer business; Amazon.com is in the on-line bookselling business, right?

Wrong! The real business of each company is the use of information.

Federal Express sells much more than delivery; it sells *confidence*.

For a customer's package or letter to "absolutely, positively" get there the next day requires a mammoth infrastructure in which the timely use of information is the key. Millions of packages, more than 600 airplanes, 40,000 trucks, and tens of thousands of employees all must be marshaled to deliver the confidence that the parcel will arrive when promised.

Using bar codes, lasers, computers, and sophisticated communications, FedEx is able to track a package's place of origination, destination, present location, and estimated time of delivery.

Fred Smith, FedEx's founder and chairman, has turned this information cache into a consumer marketing tool. By installing computer terminals in the mailing rooms of 100,000 businesses and giving proprietary software to another 650,000, FedEx has both made the customer part of its information-gathering process and improved service. Furthermore, knowing that the company gathers and maintains so much reliable information, and provides them access to it, makes customers even more confident to entrust their packages to FedEx.

The computers and software allow customers to label their own packages, calculate the charges, and notify FedEx electronically for a pickup. Even more important, the customers' ability to tap into the FedEx tracking system allows them to assure *their* customers about the delivery of vital shipments.

Information that Federal Express had to have to run its business, thus, becomes the information that enables FedEx to sell confidence to its consumers and its customers' customers.

One of the beauties of a computer-based business like Amazon.com is the information it collects about its customers. Jeff Bezos, founder of bookseller Amazon.com, uses that information to transform the on-line experience and spur sales.

Two new information technologies—"cookies" and "collaborative filtering"—are the backbone of strengthening the company's relationship with customers.

When a customer first orders from Amazon.com, a small identification code—a cookie—is placed on the customer's computer hard drive. Thereafter, every time that computer returns to the Amazon site, the cookie identifies itself to the Amazon computers as a previous customer. This allows Amazon computers to maintain a file on the orders from that user.

Using collaborative filtering, the Amazon computers project a customer's reading tastes by comparing that customer's past purchases with the purchases of others.

If someone buys a Tom Clancy novel, for instance, there is a high probability he or she will have an interest in the books purchased by other Tom Clancy fans. So, when someone who has purchased a Tom Clancy novel logs on to Amazon.com, the company's computers use collaborative filtering to recommend a list of other books culled from the purchase records of other Clancy buyers.

Amazon, thus, uses information collected by its own systems to make book shopping on the Internet an experience almost as personal as a trip to the old-fashioned neighborhood bookstore, where the person behind the counter knows your name and what you like to read.

Book superstores removed the personal touch from book buying; Amazon.com is restoring it through the use of information technology.

Using information not only makes the on-line shopping experience friendly and easy, it also drives increased sales. Having someone recommend a book they think you'll like has always been a powerful motivation to buy. Such suggestive selling worked for the neighborhood bookshop, was lost in the megastores, and is now back, thanks to Amazon's timely use of information.

As one who has used Amazon.com extensively to purchase books relevant to researching and writing this book, I can attest that Amazon's suggestive selling persuaded me to purchase Civil War books I never knew existed.

Michael Dell began selling no-name mail-order personal computers from his college dorm room in 1983. An interesting niche for a college kid, perhaps, but not much promise for the bigtime.

Who would ever buy something as complex and expensive as a computer by mail? Perhaps sight-unseen purchasing might work with a gold-plated name like IBM. But what security is there in the name Dell?

The doubters were wrong.

By 1998, the grown-up Dell was fulfilling $12 billion worth of orders annually—in large part based upon his use of information to assure consumers. The way to overcome wariness about or-dering a computer from afar, he found, was to provide the cus-tomer with a "security blanket" of information. The heart of the Dell business became a consumer-friendly information system.

The original Dell consumer information system was telephone-based. In 1992, however, Dell began pulling the plug on that way of doing business and switching to the Internet. Again, the "smart money" dismissed Dell's innovation.

"The Internet is even more impersonal than mail or phone," the skeptics warned. "Without nudging from sales reps on the phone, customers will buy less expensive systems."

Again, the doubters were wrong.

Two years after launching Dell Online, the site was producing daily sales of $6 million, almost $2 billion annually. What's more, with all the information available to Internet customers, and their ability to revisit the site again and again, they were actually buying more expensive computers on the Web than over the phone!

And they're getting better service.

"Where's my order?" is one of the questions that customers most frequently ask Dell. While the phone-based system could give a caller that information, it was not a productive use of the customer rep's time—or the customer's.

Besides, fear of being considered a pest might inhibit custom-ers from pressing for the assurances they seek. Dell's on-line cus-tomer service Web site takes the same information and makes it available any time and as many times as the customer wants to check—without tying up a phone rep.

"Dell is already on to the next big idea while companies like Compaq and IBM are still trying to catch up on its first idea," William Taylor of *Fast Company* magazine told the *Washington Post.*

That big idea is the timely use of information.

Marching Orders

The success or failure of companies and countries in the twenty-first century will be determined by the productivity of knowledge, suggests Peter Drucker.

"Knowledge" is the *use* of information.

Robert E. Lee used information. George B. McClellan collected it.

Twenty-first-century companies such as Federal Express, Dell Computer, and Amazon.com are following Robert E. Lee's model of putting information to work, quickly.

In a world in which leaders have more information available than ever before, the successful leader bears in mind the experience of George McClellan—it's not the information you have; it's how well and quickly you use it.

Lesson Seven

Small Skirmishes Decide Great Battles

The power of the individual

Every engagement can be decisive. There is no such thing as an insignificant battle. While history focuses on the grand-scale events, those milestones are nothing more than a collection of smaller engagements strung together by proximity of time and space.

The big battles and the famous generals get the headlines and the chapters in history books. Success or failure in those battles, however, rests on a cadre of lower-ranking officers and their troops.

The Battle of Gettysburg illustrates this point. A huge three-day, 160,000-man conflagration, Gettysburg's outcome was determined by leaders who never made the headlines:

• *An Indian fighter/cavalryman,* first on the field, identified the importance of the high ground behind the town and fought to preserve that ground for the Union.

• *The youngest brigade commander* in the Union army risked court martial to intercept and execute an order for someone else.

• *A college professor* hurried to the far end of the Union line to hold the position at all costs.

• *An undersized regiment of 262 Minnesotans* sacrificed

over 80 percent of its men to plug a gap in the Union line and gain five precious minutes.

The lessons of Gettysburg are equally applicable today in the marketplace battle. Companies like 3M Corporation, Southwest Airlines, and Nortel Networks have built their success by pushing leadership down the corporate hierarchy. Individuals determine victory.

The "Good Ground"
GETTYSBURG, 1863

The site of the greatest battle ever on the North American continent was a happenstance of the layout of the Pennsylvania road network.

In mid-1863, Robert E. Lee's Army of Northern Virginia was once again taking the war to the farms and families of the North. The Rebel army was in Pennsylvania. When word reached him that Union forces were moving to confront his invasion, Lee ordered his dispersed Confederate army to reassemble. From as far as Harrisburg to the north and Chambersburg to the west, the Confederates took to the roads, heading for a linkup.

Meanwhile, from Frederick, Maryland, to the south, Federal troops were moving on the same road network, searching for the Rebels.

The web of roads met at a small, prosperous town called Gettysburg.

At the forefront of the Union advance, probing for the location of the enemy, rode two cavalry brigades commanded by thirty-seven-year-old Brigadier General John Buford. Six months later this West Pointer, who had earned his spurs fighting Indians in the West prior to the Civil War, would be dead of "exposure and exhaustion," a testament to his driven style of command.

Arriving at Gettysburg the day before the great battle began, Buford immediately saw how the convergence of eleven roads would draw in the opposing armies. Since he was the first on the scene, it fell to Buford to determine the early strategy that would set the stage for all that followed.

"It was Buford who selected the battlefield where the two armies were about to measure their strength," wrote the Comte de Paris in his *History of the Civil War in America.* "Neither Meade nor Lee had any knowledge of it . . . Buford, who when he arrived on the evening of [June] 30th, had guessed at one glance the advantages to be derived from these positions, did not have time to give a description of them to Meade and receive his instructions."

In other words, independent of his superiors, John Buford assumed the responsibility for carrying out the first, vital Union maneuver of the battle—to prevent the converging Confederates from occupying the most advantageous positions.

"By daylight of July 1," Buford wrote in his report, "I had gained positive information of the enemy's position and movements, and my arrangements were made for entertaining him until General Reynolds [and his I Corps Infantry] could reach the scene."

Instead of placing his troopers on the high ground east and south of town—a logical defensive position, but one that would draw the Rebels' superior strength to the heights at the very outset—Buford deployed his men on the opposite side of the village, where they could hopefully delay the Confederate advance until the approaching Union infantry could occupy the heights.

To accomplish this, Buford planned a defense that ran along ridges that intersected the main route from the west at almost right angles.

Not everyone shared Buford's vision. The night before the battle, in response to one of his brigade commanders' expression of doubt that the Rebels would attack, Buford anticipated the first few hours of the first day of the Battle of Gettysburg.

"They will attack you in the morning and they will come booming—skirmishers three-deep. You will have to fight like the devil until support arrives."

Indeed, at five-thirty the next morning, July 1, 1863, the Confederate advance came into contact with Buford's troops almost four miles west of Gettysburg.

Buford ordered his cavalrymen to dismount from their horses and fight on the ground—an old Indian tactic. Every fourth trooper held the steeds of three dismounted comrades. From behind fences and posts Buford's troopers fought a delaying action.

Their effort against superior Confederate numbers was greatly assisted by their better weapons. Whereas an advancing Rebel soldier could, optimally, get off four rounds a minute from his muzzle-loader, the Union troops were equipped with seven-shot carbines that could deliver twenty rounds a minute.

By about 8 A.M., Buford's men were in a battle line along Herr Ridge. For two hours they held off the larger Confederate force. Finally, they dropped back and resumed their stand atop the next rise, McPherson's Ridge, approximately one mile from the western edge of the town. Buford's troopers held this new position for another two hours—1,600 Federal cavalry stopping 3,800 Confederate infantry.

At about the time that Buford was falling back on McPherson's Ridge, Union Major General John Reynolds arrived on the field in advance of his I Corps. Reynolds immediately recognized the value of the heights east and south of Gettysburg that Buford had been fighting to preserve.

"The enemy are advancing in strong force . . . I fear they will get to the heights beyond the town before I can," Reynolds messaged Union commander Major General George Meade.

But, in the opposite of the Hollywood cliché, Reynold's infantry arrived just in the nick of time to save Buford's cavalry!

For the next two days, Robert E. Lee tried to dislodge Federal forces from the high ground that Buford had fought so providentially and tenaciously to deny to the Rebels. The Confederates never were able to take possession of the heights.

Instead, the high ground became the Union army's greatest advantage, the bequest of John Buford's foresight.

By his independent action, a little-known brigade commander, John Buford, had determined the character of the Battle of Gettysburg and, thus, shaped its outcome.

THE BATTLE FOR LITTLE ROUND TOP

Because of the good work of John Buford and his troopers, the evening and night of July 1 found Union troops filling in a fishhook-shaped position along the heights east and south of the town. The barb of the hook was at Culp's Hill and the shank ran through Cemetery Hill and Ridge, with the south end at the hills known as the Round Tops.

Late in the afternoon of July 2, Robert E. Lee's men attacked the lower shank of the fishhook.

While Confederate units engaged their foes along the shank of the fishhook, Rebel Colonel William Oates' brigade of two Alabama regiments tried to slide around the Union left flank. After taking the larger, southernmost of these two hills, Big Round Top, without opposition, Oates was ordered to move up the fishhook and take Little Round Top.

Big Round Top's summit was heavily wooded and, as such, of little value to either side as a base of operations. Little Round Top, however, featured a clear summit presently being used to advantage as a Union observation and signaling station.

If the Confederates could place artillery atop Little Round Top, they would be able to rake the Union line with shot and shell. Even more important, such a position would place the Rebels on the Union flank, capable of attacking the Federal line at its most vulnerable point and "rolling up" the Union forces much as Jackson had done at Chancellorsville (see Lesson Five).

And at that critical moment, the priceless real estate of Little Round Top was virtually empty of Union defenders!

The Young Colonel

The Union chief of engineers, Brigadier General Gouverneur K. Warren, was operating that day as the alter ego of Union commander Major General George C. Meade. While inspecting the Federal flank, Warren discovered the void on Little Round Top—a void that was especially worrisome when, from its summit, he saw Rebel troops advancing in line of battle only a mile away to the west.

The strategically crucial position was occupied by only a handful of Union signal corps officers sending semaphore signals. Warren sent word of this vulnerability to General Meade, then galloped down the hill toward the advancing Rebels in search of Federal troops to fill the void.

Major General George Sykes and his Union V Corps had just arrived on the battlefield. Having been personally instructed by Meade to reinforce the Union left, Sykes had marched his men over Cemetery Ridge to a position where they were now between the advancing Graybacks and the Union high ground.

When Warren informed him of the situation, Sykes immediately dispatched orders to Brigadier General James Barnes, the oldest division commander in the army, to move parts of his 1st Division to occupy Little Round Top.

The messenger, a lieutenant on Sykes' staff, could not locate General Barnes on the battlefield.

Twenty-six-year-old Colonel Strong Vincent, the youngest brigade commander in the Union army, intercepted the messenger.

"What are your orders?" he inquired. The lieutenant carrying the instructions was reluctant to break the chain of command—his orders were to deliver the message to General Barnes, not to some young colonel. However, the pre-war lawyer refused to be intimidated.

"Give me your orders!" commanded the youthful Vincent. Finally and reluctantly, the messenger revealed the order's contents—Barnes was to send a brigade to occupy "yonder hill."

Immediately Vincent saw the importance of "yonder hill"—Little Round Top—and assumed the orders for himself.

Looking back on Vincent's decision from the perspective of time, his action seems logical and almost preordained. On July 2, 1863, however, the decision was flirting with court-martial.

The young colonel, less than three weeks past his twenty-sixth birthday, had inserted himself between his superior and his superior's superior, violating the command structure and substituting his judgment for that of the generals above him. And by doing so, Vincent was separating his brigade from its division without permission, potentially threatening both.

Without wasting valuable minutes looking for General Barnes, Colonel Vincent ordered his bugler to sound advance and rushed his 1,350 men on the "double quick" away from the battle building in his sector and up the western slope of Little Round Top.

Riding ahead of his men, Vincent reconnoitered the hill. Fearing that placing his men on the crest would make it easier for the Rebels to work their way around his flank, Vincent determined to make his stand on the slope of Little Round Top.

The first Federal unit to reach Little Round Top was the 20th Maine Regiment, commanded by Colonel Joshua Lawrence Chamberlain. The men from Maine climbed the western face of the hill and stumbled over its summit down the southern slope to find their brigade commander waiting.

"I place you here," Vincent told Chamberlain. "This is the left of the Union line. You understand? You are to hold this ground at all costs."

It was the last command Vincent would ever give Chamberlain. Leaving Chamberlain on his own, Vincent returned to the western face of the hill to oversee its defense. A few minutes later the young colonel was shot through the heart by a rebel bullet.

"If any one brigade saved George G. Meade's army at Gettysburg, it was Vincent's," observed Ezra Warner's *Generals in*

Blue. Strong Vincent's independent action to carry out the orders intended for someone else was not only the young man's last full measure, it quite possibly saved the Union army.

The Professor

Just a year prior, thirty-five-year-old Joshua Chamberlain, the man to whom Vincent entrusted the end of the Union flank, had been a professor of rhetoric and revealed religion at Maine's Bowdoin College. When the college refused to release him to fight in the war, Chamberlain left for a "sabbatical" and enlisted anyway.

Now, he commanded the most vulnerable position of the Union line in the greatest battle thus far in the war.

No sooner had Chamberlain placed his men in defensive positions on Little Round Top than the Rebels began their assault. The battle raged for hours.

"The edge of the fight swayed back and forth like a wave," Chamberlain wrote. "At times I saw around me more of the enemy than of my own men."

The Rebels would charge and be forced back, only to move to their right and charge again. The fighting was intense as the approximately 300 men of Chamberlain's Maine Regiment (plus 100 or so mutineers they had been assigned to guard) held off the superior Confederate force.

"Thick groups in gray were pushing . . . to gain our left flank," Chamberlain wrote. "If they could hold our attention by a hot fight in front while they got in force on that flank, it would be bad for us and our whole defense."

Conventional military tactics suggest that in such circumstances the appropriate move would have been to face about and form a new, tighter line higher up the hill. Chamberlain, however, was not a conventional soldier. As the Rebs kept moving to his left, Chamberlain thinned his ranks from two to one man deep and extended the line, "refusing" it (i.e., turning it at a right angle to the existing line) so as to protect his own flank.

Pushed by unremitting pressure from Colonel William Oates' Alabama regiments to flank him, Chamberlain found that his position at the end of the Union line had almost become a "U." In other words, he was virtually surrounded by Rebels, forced to defend himself against assaults from all angles. At times, men in blue and gray were fighting hand-to-hand.

"Three times our line was forced back, but only to rally and repulse the enemy," Chamberlain wrote. "As often as the enemy's line was broken and routed, a new [Confederate] line was unmasked which advanced with fresh vigor."

One-third of the 20th Maine had been incapacitated by the Confederate attacks—killed or wounded. The survivors scavenged among the bodies of the fallen for ammunition. Even after scavenging, however, Chamberlain's men were soon running out of bullets.

"Only a desperate chance was left for us," Chamberlain recognized.

As the Confederates fell back briefly, the Maine professor shouted the command, "Bayonets!" and led his men down the hill straight at the Confederates. Knocked off balance and caught by surprise, the first rank of Confederates surrendered. As those further back began to retreat, Chamberlain's Company B, which had been detached to guard against a wide Rebel flanking move, pounced on them.

Chamberlain's bayonet charge broke the back of the Confederate assault.

"When the battle commenced, four hours previously," explained Confederate Colonel Oates, "I had the strongest and finest regiment in Hood's Division. Its effectives numbered nearly 700 officers and men. Now 225 answered at roll-call, and more than half of my officers had been left on the field."

Two civilians-turned-soldiers—a twenty-six-year-old lawyer and a thirty-five-year-old college professor—had saved the vulnerable Union flank on Little Round Top through independent judgment and resolute action.

After the war, Confederate Lieutenant General James Longstreet, who had commanded the Rebel offensive that day, told a gathering of Union veterans just how close the Federals had come to having their flank turned. "I was three minutes late in occupying Little Round Top. If I had got there first, you would have had as much trouble getting rid of me as I did trying to get rid of you."

Colonel Strong Vincent's independent action gave the Union those precious minutes. Colonel Joshua Chamberlain's stubborn defense preserved them. Together, they may have preserved the Union as well.

The First Minnesota Saves the Day

As the action on Little Round Top wound to a close, the battle continued further up the shank of the fishhook. The Confederates were attacking "en echelon," a tactic by which a unit attacks only after the one next to it has advanced. Thus, after Major General John B. Hood's division began attacking the southern end of the Union line by the Round Tops, Major General Lafayette McLaws' division began an attack further north along the Union line.

McLaws' advance discovered the Federals in a surprisingly vulnerable position. Thanks to the military ineptitude of its political general, Daniel Sickles, the Union III Corps was strung out almost a half mile in front of Cemetery Ridge's high ground, separated from and far in advance of the rest of the Union forces.

Major General Sickles, a Tammany Hall Democratic congressman before the war, had not liked his assigned position along Cemetery Ridge. On his own authority, Sickles moved his line so that it angled out from Cemetery Ridge to a peach orchard a half mile distant. By creating this salient, Sickles left both his flanks unconnected to the main Union force and recklessly thinned his line in order to cover a greater distance.

Foolhardy and impetuous action was nothing new to Dan Sickles. Before the war, while a Member of Congress, he had killed his wife's lover, the son of Francis Scott Key. Sickles escaped punishment, though, becoming the first person ever acquitted of murder by reason of temporary insanity.

At Gettysburg, the victims of Sickles' foolhardy action were his corps, himself (he was wounded and carried from the field), and the 1st Minnesota Regiment.

At the point in the Union line assigned to Sickles, Cemetery Ridge virtually disappears, becoming a gradual 200-yard slope down to Plum Run, a rocky-banked creek which was dry at that time of year. By angling his line forward across Plum Run, Sickles opened the opportunity for his troops to be assailed from three sides simultaneously.

Two Confederate brigades were only too happy to seize that opportunity. After intense fighting at the peach orchard, the Federal troops fell back into a wheat field between the orchard and Plum Run. The fighting became even more intense and possession of the wheat field changed hands six times.

The numerically superior Confederate troops finally broke through and pushed Sickles' Union forces across Plum Run and up the incline to Cemetery Ridge.

The breakthrough opened the door to a potential disaster for the Federals. Because of Sickles' unauthorized advance, there was a gap at this point in the Union line. If the Rebels could exploit that gap and pour through into the Union rear, they could then simply roll up the exposed Federal flanks in either direction.

Disaster was imminent as a brigade of 1,600 Confederate soldiers charged up the slope to break the Federal line.

Union Major General Winfield Scott Hancock, now commanding both his own II Corps as well as replacing the wounded Sickles as the head of III Corps, sent for reserves. But there was not enough time for the reserves to reach the scene. The Rebs were already coming up the slope.

Nothing stood between the 1,600 charging Confederates and a breakthrough to the Union rear but the 262 men of the 1st Minnesota Regiment.

"My God," exclaimed Hancock, "are these all the men we have here?"

The general saw his tactical problem all too clearly. Somehow he needed to hold off the charging Confederates for a brief period of time until Union reinforcements could arrive.

"I saw that in some way five minutes must be gained or we were lost," Hancock later explained.

"Colonel, do you see those colors?" Hancock inquired of the Minnesotans' commander, Colonel William Colvill, pointing to the advancing Confederates. "Then take them!"

"Every man realized in an instant what the order meant," wrote the regiment's adjutant, "death or wounds to us all; the sacrifice of the regiment to gain a few minutes and save the position, and probably the battlefield—and every man saw and accepted the necessity for the sacrifice."

Ordering his men to fix their bayonets, Colonel Colvill stepped in front and ordered, "Forward, double-quick!"

Down the slope charged the 1st Minnesota Regiment. Three times the regimental colors fell only to be picked up again. By the time the regiment reached Plum Run, a quarter of the men had fallen. Now, only twenty-five or thirty yards away, the Rebels poured volley after volley into the Minnesotans. But Colonel Colvill's men kept coming, not yet having fired a shot.

And, as one member of the regiment wrote later, "The men were never made who will stand against leveled bayonets coming with such momentum and evident desperation."

The first rank of Confederates broke in the face of the onrushing bayonets and fell back upon the second rank. The Rebel advance stopped.

Only then did the Minnesotans open fire. Jumping behind the rocks on the creek bank, the Union troops began firing individually and in small groups. Approximately 150 men had made it this far—now the job was to hold on against a Confederate force ten times larger.

For fifteen minutes the remnants of the regiment clung to the bank of Plum Run. Just as the Rebels were enveloping their position, the Union reinforcements arrived.

The day had been saved. What was left of the 1st Minnesota withdrew.

A handful of men had stopped the charge of a Confederate brigade and plugged the hole in the vital center of the Union line. General Hancock had asked the Minnesotans to buy him five minutes. They delivered much more than that, and, in the process, saved the Union line.

But at what a price!

Of the 262 men who initially stepped off in the 1st Minnesota bayonet charge, 229 fell dead or wounded—a staggering 87 percent. The 1st Minnesota suffered the highest percentage of casualties of any Union regiment in a single engagement in the entire war.

"In all the history of warfare, this charge has few, if any, equals and no superiors," Calvin Coolidge observed in 1909. "It was an exhibition of the most exalted heroism against an apparently insuperable antagonist. By holding the Confederate force in check until other reserves came up, it probably saved the Union army from defeat . . . So far as human judgment can determine, Colonel Colvill and those eight companies of the First Minnesota are entitled to rank among the saviors of their country."

Planes, Phones, and Post-its

In the corporate world, encouraging the kind of individual leadership exhibited at Gettysburg is known as "empowerment."

The phenomenal success of the 3M Corporation's Post-it Notes is an example of the benefits such a policy can bring. The corporate philosophy at 3M, in fact, encourages—nay, *demands*—innovative contributions not just from its corporate generals but from the colonels, captains, and sergeants, all the way down to the privates.

Taking over the struggling Minnesota Mining and Manufacturing Company during World War I, accountant-turned-sales-manager-turned-general-manager William McKnight bombarded his small staff with maxims designed to stimulate a constant flow of new and successful product ideas:

"Hire good people and leave them alone."

"Listen to anyone with an original idea, no matter how absurd it might sound at first."

"Encourage, don't nitpick. Let people run with an idea."

Eight decades later this philosophy continues to prevail. A company rule allows 3M's 8,000 researchers to devote 15 percent of their work time to their own pet projects, unrelated to their official assignments and without approval of their supervisor.

Called "bootlegging," this policy has kept 3M innovative and growing, producing, for instance, one of the most ubiquitous ideas of modern life.

One Sunday in 1974, while singing in his church choir, 3M employee Art Fry grappled with a simple problem. "To make it easier to find the songs we were going to sing, I used to mark the places with little slips of paper," he recalled. But the slips would frequently fall out, causing him to lose his place. "Gee, if I had a little adhesive on these bookmarks, that would be just the ticket."

Back in the office, Art wandered over to visit a friend, Spence Silver, working in another lab. There he learned that Silver had concocted a nonbinding adhesive by mixing together a bunch of chemicals "just to see what would happen."

Bingo! Fry slapped some of Silver's stick-um on a little piece of paper and Post-it Notes were born. The brightly colored squares are today found stuck everywhere—thanks to Fry and Silver "bootlegging" instead of waiting for the higher-ups (and their market consultants) to tell them what to do.

The empowerment of employees has achieved almost religious fervor at Southwest Airlines, America's premier no-frills, low-cost airline. Herb Kelleher, Southwest's Chairman/CEO, dares to utter the unorthodox opinion that his employees are more important than his customers.

Kelleher believes that the phenomenal success of Southwest is based on selectively hiring motivated workers compatible with the company's culture, training them to do their jobs with warmth, friendliness, and a sense of fun—and then letting them make decisions.

"Take the organization pyramid and turn it upside down," Kelleher explained to *Management Review* magazine. "Turn it on its point. Down here, at the bottom, you've got the people at headquarters. Up there, at the top, you've got the people who are there in the field, on the front lines. They're the ones who make things happen. They're the experts. You can compare our roles in the office to the military. We're the supply corps. We're not the heroes. We supply the heroes, period. The heroes are out there."

The selection of new employees to work in this environment is itself an exercise in empowerment. After being interviewed in groups to see how they interact with peers, applicants are sized up by their future colleagues, not just by the human resources department. Once hired, the new workers must serve a probation period to make sure they fit into the Southwest culture.

"You may be an excellent performer, but incompatible with our culture here," Kelleher explains. "It doesn't mean there's anything wrong with you, there's just not a match."

And how does Southwest know if an employee is meeting its standards and thriving in its culture? By paying attention to letters of complaint from passengers. Kelleher claims to read every letter and every employee evaluation.

If a worker is the target of passenger complaints, "we don't tell employees what to do about it," Kelleher relates. "That's up to them. But we let them know there's a problem that needs fixing."

While Herb Kelleher built his company through empowerment, John Roth saved his in the nick of time by getting the generals out of the way.

In 1992, Northern Telecom (now known as Nortel Networks) was enjoying record profit increases. At the same time, the company was in deep trouble. The then-CEO ruled with an iron hand, focusing on short-term profits at the expense of research and development and other future-oriented efforts.

As a result, Nortel was stuck in the unexciting niche of manufacturing switching equipment for wireline telephone companies at the time when the telecommunications industry was exploding with new technologies and new ventures.

Nortel had no presence in the new wireless business, nor in high-speed networks, nor in intelligent networks. Focusing on cost cutting, Nortel had both limited its opportunities and affected its product quality.

Then, in 1993, the bottom fell out. A bug in Nortel's switching software disrupted service for telephone companies and their customers.

John Roth was brought in as CEO to clean up the mess. Under his leadership, a new corporate culture began to take shape. All wisdom didn't reside at headquarters anymore. Decisions were pushed down the corporate ladder to employees closer to the customers and their needs.

Roth recalled in a *New York Times* interview that under the old micro-management system, corporate headquarters dictated to all the business units.

"How we got to be so smart at corporate that we knew how much R&D you need is a mystery," Roth confessed to a reporter. "Now . . . we say, 'This is how much earnings we need from you. You figure out how to do that.' That allowed these units to operate more like small companies."

"The people who make the decisions are the ones facing the customer," Matt Desch, president of Nortel's wireless networks division, told *Electronic Business* magazine.

On Desch's initiative, for instance, Nortel Wireless spent $415 million to acquire Broadband Networks Inc. and the technology Desch believed was essential if Nortel was going to be a player in the new microwave-based wireless telecommunications services.

"I went to the board, said I've talked to customers and know what I need for my business, and they said, 'Go for it,'" Desch recalls. "I negotiated for two weeks, the due diligence took days. From start to finish the deal took a month and a half."

Empowering the troops away from headquarters transformed Nortel Networks into one of the most innovative and fast-moving companies in the brutally innovative and fast-moving telecommunications industry.

Marching Orders

"You win with people," I used to hear legendary Ohio State football coach Woody Hayes preach in recognition of the importance of the individual in a team victory.

Because the greatest of struggles is but the sum of its parts, there are no small roles nor insignificant engagements. Victory on a grand scale is the result of the small victories of individuals who have been given an objective and empowered to make the necessary decisions to achieve it.

Lesson Eight

To Be a Leader, You Must Lead

Courage of conviction

Football coaches call it a gut check. At a crucial moment, leaders must rely on something beyond their intellect, beyond their factual analysis of the situation. That something has to come from within.

Civil War generals taught us that at the heart of leadership lies conviction. The leaders in the war had to call upon a reserve of courage. Physical courage, quite certainly, but also personal courage built upon a deep conviction.

Ulysses S. Grant had it in spades and tried to instill it in those he commanded. Confederates Robert E. Lee and John Bell Hood likewise led through a display of conviction.

The antithesis of these generals in the Civil War was Union Major General Ambrose Burnside. When Burnside reached deep down to find his wellspring of conviction, the cup repeatedly came up dry.

Telecommunications tycoon Craig McCaw built the nation's largest cellular telephone network upon the conviction that he was fulfilling a human longing, to communicate free of technological limitation, as well as building a business. Today, McCaw continues to build the next generation of telecommunications services out of an even broader conviction.

Conviction separates leaders from pretenders.

Grant and Lee
THE WILDERNESS, 1864

In March 1864, President Lincoln, frustrated yet again by a string of irresolute Federal generals, gave overall command of Union forces to U. S. Grant, the hero of Vicksburg.

Recognizing the importance of breaking the back of the rebellion by breaking Robert E. Lee's Army of Northern Virginia, Grant chose to make his headquarters in the field with the Army of the Potomac, the Union force confronting Lee.

Technically, Grant left command of that army in the hands of Major General George G. Meade. But when the boss pitches his tent next to yours, it's clear who's in charge.

By the first week of May, Grant had the Union army in motion—heading south. When asked by a reporter how long it would take him to reach Richmond, Grant replied, "I will agree to be there in about four days. That is, if General Lee becomes party to the arrangement. But if he objects, the trip will undoubtedly be prolonged."

The first challenge the Union army faced was traversing the area known as the Wilderness. Only thirteen months prior, Lee had chased the same Union army from the same area at the Battle of Chancellorsville (see Lesson Five).

The aptly named Wilderness was a jungle of scrub brush and second-growth trees which had sprung up thickly after the original forest was cut down to feed the iron smelter furnaces throughout the region. Only a few roads led through the wild and untamed Wilderness. The Union army's advantages of superior numbers and artillery were nullified by the dense growth, which restricted maneuver and eliminated clear fields of fire for the Federal cannon. Grant expected his army to sprint through this obstacle in just two days in order to break out into the open where his full weight could be brought to bear on Lee's forces.

Grant's new command, however, was not composed of sprinters. The Union soldiers weren't used to the kind of speed and responsiveness that Grant demanded. The march came to a halt in the midst of the Wilderness so that a potentially dangerous gap could be closed between the lead divisions and Major General Ambrose Burnside's IX Corps, which was charged with protecting the rear.

Lee's Army of Northern Virginia was a jackrabbit in comparison. The Confederate troops sprang into action as soon as their commander saw that Grant was heading south.

Early on the second full day of Grant's march—while still in the Wilderness—Union forces encountered the Confederates.

Ulysses Grant had come to fight. His commitment was to the destruction of the Confederate force that had bedeviled six previous Union commanders over the last three years.

When reports reached him during breakfast on May 5 that the Union's advance division had run into Rebels in its path, Grant told Meade, "If any opportunity presents itself for pitching into a part of Lee's Army, do so without giving [Lee] time for disposition."

Major General Gouverneur K. Warren, commanding the lead corps of the Union army, unfortunately did not share Grant's sense of urgency, and it was early afternoon before his troops finally "pitched into" the Rebels.

The delay gave Lee the opportunity to rush more troops to the site of the impending confrontation. When Warren finally attacked, he faced a reinforced opponent who made full use of the inhospitable landscape. Federal superiority, however, finally began to prevail and only nightfall stopped a Union breakthrough.

Grant gave instructions for the assault to resume at first light the following day.

"Lee to the rear!"

As planned, the Union troops attacked at 5 A.M. on May 6, the overwhelming Federal force throwing itself against a strangely unprepared Confederate division. Emerging from the woods, the Bluecoats charged across the clearing of the Widow Tapp's farm. The only thing preventing a Confederate rout was an artillery battery that poured canister shells into the advancing Union ranks, briefly buying time.

But the Rebel division commander, Major General A. P. Hill, was oddly unfocused on the impending disaster. He failed to order his men to dig in during the night, and when the Union attack began at dawn, they would pay the price for his unpreparedness.

When the fighting started, Hill seemed incapable of exercising effective command control of his division. Robert E. Lee, who was on the battlefield at that moment, stepped in and began providing tactical leadership, which normally would have been the domain of Hill.

Lee knew that somewhere to his rear was the Confederate I Corps, commanded by Lieutenant General James Longstreet. If those reinforcements did not arrive with dispatch, however, the day would be lost. Suddenly, in the nick of time, men in gray started appearing from the Rebel rear.

"General, what brigade is this?" Lee asked the officer in the lead.

"The Texas Brigade," was the reply.

"I wish you to give those [Union] men cold steel—they will stand and fire all day, and never move unless you charge them," Lee commanded the arriving reinforcements.

As the Texas Brigade assembled for the attack, Lee rose in the stirrups of his gray horse, Traveller, in front of the troops, waving his hat, and shouting, "Texans always move them . . ."

Then the aristocratic Lee began to advance with the troops, urging the men forward.

With Union bullets whizzing dangerously close, Lee's staff tried to persuade him to retreat to a safer position. Staff officers seized the reins of his horse. They grabbed at the commanding general's arms. But to no avail. Lee shook them off, continuing to place himself in harm's way, advancing with his troops.

As the Texas soldiers realized that their beloved leader had placed himself in grave danger, they slowed their advance and began to shout, "Lee to the rear! We won't go on unless you go back."

At last, the Confederate commander accepted the need to remove himself to a safer place. Lee wheeled his horse around and rode to the rear to consult with General Longstreet.

The scene would be repeated no less than five times within the next seven days. Lee was physically and emotionally energized by the courage of his convictions. Only his men's insistence that he seek safety—"Lee to the rear!"—could break the grip those convictions had on his actions.

Grant Teaches Conviction

On the other side of the line, U. S. Grant was engaged in a different form of leadership—a battlefield assessment of the capabilities of his new subordinates, a bit of lesson-teaching to a group of officers who, while not lacking courage, had demonstrated insufficient conviction.

"In previous battles," Geoffrey Perret observed in *Ulysses S. Grant,* "his command style was urgent and direct . . . His habit was to swing himself into the saddle without a word, then ride off at top speed to where the fighting was hottest."

That style, so successful at Shiloh and elsewhere, would not work now. Only a few weeks previously, Grant had inherited a new command structure and a new set of subordinate officers. He had to learn about them firsthand, to discover why the smaller, ill-equipped Rebel army had so often vanquished them.

What was the essential ingredient of success that the leadership of the Union army lacked?

In order to discern the answer to that question, Grant was uncharacteristically forced to observe rather than participate. While the battle raged in the Wilderness, Grant nervously hacked away at small pieces of wood with a pocketknife and puffed at a cigar. By the end of the first day of the Battle of the Wilderness, his knife had slashed great gashes in his new riding gloves and he had consumed twenty stogies.

There was plenty for Grant to worry about. The initial Union early morning advance had been stopped and Longstreet's Confederate reinforcements were attacking the Federal flank. The day, which had started with such promise, was beginning to turn against Grant.

Then the Union commander caught an unexpected break. General Longstreet, returning from scouting his flanking maneuver, was shot accidentally by his own men.

History seemed to be repeating itself. Just thirteen months before, a few miles away, Stonewall Jackson had led a similar flanking movement only to suffer a similar fate at the hands of his own troops. (Unlike Jackson, Longstreet would survive his wounds. However, he would be out of action for many months.) With Longstreet down, the Confederate advance stalled.

At the opposite end of the Confederate line, Rebel Brigadier General John B. Gordon had been agitating all day for permission to attack Grant's northern flank, which, he had discovered, was isolated, unattached to other supporting Union forces.

Finally unleashed at the end of the day, Gordon's Confederates fell upon Major General John Sedgwick's VI Corps, surprising them. Over 500 Federals were quickly taken prisoner, including two brigade commanders.

One of Sedgwick's officers came flying into Union headquarters to announce that Sedgwick was dead and his corps routed.

"I don't believe it," replied Grant.

Troops were shifted to reinforce the Union's exposed northern flank. Still, reports of disaster continued to arrive at the Federal headquarters.

Was this what it had been like during the previous three years—hard-fought battles lost because the Union generals had lost their nerve at decisive moments?

Finally, one officer, upset that Grant did not appear to be taking the situation seriously, felt compelled to relate the Union army's previous experience to explain the current peril.

"I know Lee's methods well by past experience," this officer told the new commander. "He will throw his whole army between us and the Rapidan [River], and cut us off completely from our communications."

That did it. Grant exploded.

"I am heartily tired of hearing about what Lee is going to do," Grant barked. "Some of you always seem to think he is suddenly going to turn a double somersault and land in our rear and on both our flanks at the same time. Go back to your command and try to think about what we are going to do ourselves, instead of what Lee is going to do!"

Ulysses S. Grant was teaching his army a new concept—the courage of their convictions. New to the Army of the Potomac, drawn into a battle where he had hoped to avoid engagement, having suffered in two days casualties greater than the same army's ignominious defeat a year earlier at Chancellorsville, Grant was delivering the message that he intended to prevail, and that his subordinates were expected to deliver that victory.

That evening, to a reporter on his way to Washington, Grant said, "If you see the President, tell him that whatever happens, there will be no turning back."

The next day, Grant gave orders that the Union army would

not withdraw, but would maneuver and move south to again engage the Confederates, exhibiting the courage of his convictions, and demanding that his subordinates do the same.

The Antithesis of Leadership
AMBROSE BURNSIDE

U. S. Grant could reach inside himself at crucial moments during the Civil War to summon the courage needed to make vital decisions. That trait was absent in most of the generals Grant inherited—but in none was it more lacking than in Major General Ambrose Burnside.

Burnside's abundant whiskers contributed the term "sideburns" to our lexicon. Beyond that, his Civil War legacy was to be at the right place at the right time with the wrong leadership.

That Burnside had physical courage was not in doubt. As a leader, however, he lacked the kind of instinctive gut conviction that Grant relied on for decision-making. In its place, Burnside substituted stubbornness. Both courage and stubbornness can be useful qualities in a leader. But they cannot make up for lack of conviction. Without such conviction, Burnside had difficulty making decisions in rapidly changing battlefield situations. And that lack of decisiveness cost Ambrose Burnside many battles. It cost many of his soldiers their lives.

As much as anyone, Ambrose Burnside was responsible for the bloodiest day of the Civil War, the Battle of Antietam (Sharpsburg). Given responsibility for the left wing of the Union army (see Lesson One), Burnside's job was to lead his men across Antietam Creek to assault the Confederate right. Somehow Burnside got it into his head that he had to use a stone bridge to cross the creek.

That bridge still stands today, a silent monument to a leader who, when it came time for decisive commitment, was running on empty.

On the Union side, the road leading to the bridge ran parallel to Antietam Creek for a couple hundred yards before making a sharp turn across the span. On the Confederate side, high ground gave Rebel riflemen a clean shot at the Bluecoats as they moved down that two-hundred-yard stretch of road.

Because Burnside insisted on marching his men to the bridge along the exposed road, 450 Georgians were able to hold off 14,000 Federals for a crucial seven hours.

The water in the creek was only about four feet deep and the creek was only fifty feet wide. Burnside's troops could easily have waded across without getting their whiskers wet. Likewise, the road was not the only approach to the bridge. The surrounding fields provided a much less risky route.

But Burnside, substituting stubbornness for decisiveness, sacrificed men in a vain and misguided effort to use the approach road and the bridge.

Robert E. Lee, pleasantly surprised at the gift the bullheaded Burnside had given him on his right, was able to remove Confederate troops from that sector in order to shore up other parts of the Confederate line. The Rebel troops freed up by the ineptitude and indecisiveness of Ambrose Burnside made the difference in the battle by plugging holes in the Confederate line as the superior Union force pummeled it elsewhere.

Finally, around one o'clock in the afternoon, Burnside gave up the murderous road approach and sent two regiments across the fields straight at the bridge over Antietam Creek. The tactic worked. At last, the Union army was across the creek and attacking Lee's right flank.

But having crossed the creek, the ever-indecisive Burnside stopped. Faced with a minuscule force of Confederates, Burnside waited while a new Union division came up to replace his lead division, which had exhausted its ammunition during the seven hours it exchanged fire with the rebels across the Antietam. It was 3 P.M. before Burnside ordered his troops to move against the Confederate flank.

The two delays—at the bridge and after the crossing—allowed a miraculous deliverance for the Confederates. Just as Burnside's troops finally began to move, Rebel General A. P. Hill's division—straight from a seventeen-mile forced march from Harpers Ferry—surged onto the battlefield and routed the Federals.

If not for Burnside's failure of decisive action at Antietam, his troops could have waded the creek and rolled over the Confederates hours before Hill's arrival.

But Burnside's failure of leadership at Antietam paled in comparison to that of his friend and overall Union commander General George B. McClellan. When Lincoln removed McClellan for not moving quickly to exploit the Confederate retreat from Antietam, the President chose Ambrose Burnside as the new head of the Army of the Potomac.

Lincoln sacked McClellan because he was not aggressive enough. Burnside determined that if it was aggressiveness Lincoln wanted, it was aggressiveness he would deliver.

Immediately the Union army began moving. By mid-November 1862, the 120,000-man force was halfway between Washington and Richmond, ready to cross the Rappahannock River opposite Fredericksburg, Virginia, on the road to the Confederate capital.

Then his Achilles' heel tripped up Burnside again. Pontoon bridges needed to carry his men across the river were delayed. They would not arrive until a week after the planned date. As a result, Lee's forces were able to anticipate the Federal crossing and prepare to repel the advance.

Lee used the delay to place his men on the heights behind Fredericksburg and for five miles down the Rappahannock. Putting himself in his opponent's shoes, Lee expected Burnside to slide southward and try another crossing downriver.

Burnside, in fact, had evolved just such a plan, a sliding strategy not unlike that successfully pursued by Grant sixteen months later.

However, there was intense political pressure on Burnside from Washington to attack, not maneuver.

A leader with conviction and the courage to stick with it would have assessed the new developments—the delay in the arrival of the pontoon bridges giving Lee time to prepare a strong defense—and made the appropriate revisions, moving his crossing downriver, away from the Confederate defenses, ignoring the demands of the politicians.

Without the conviction to stand up to the political pressure, however, Burnside determined to carry out his original plan and await the arrival of the pontoon bridges to cross at Fredericksburg.

Again, stubbornness in place of conviction. It was the bridge at Antietam all over again.

The night before the attack, Burnside described his plan in a telegram to Washington, adding a wistful "We hope to succeed."

Perhaps in those four words Ambrose Burnside was revealing his innermost recognition that stubbornness is no substitute for the conviction to do what he knew was really necessary.

Unfortunately his hope wasn't good enough.

Burnside's men crossed the Rappahannock on the late-arriving pontoon bridges, but well-prepared Rebel defenders atop Marye's Heights, concealed behind a stone wall and in a sunken road, were ready for them.

The hill atop which the Confederates sat was on the far side of town from the river. Once the Union troops had forced their way through Confederate delaying actions in Fredericksburg, they had to assault the Rebel positions across an open field.

The approach was targeted by so many Confederate artillery pieces that one Rebel gunner told his commander, "General, we cover that ground now so well that we comb it as with a fine tooth comb. A chicken could not live on that field when we open on it."

Into that maelstrom Burnside sent the Army of the Potomac.

As historian Shelby Foote explained in his classic *The Civil War*, "The new commander, in the face of all those guns across the river, seemed to believe it was part of his duty to expose his army to annihilation by way of payment for other men's mistakes."

What happened to Burnside's men on the slope leading up from the river to Marye's Heights was a slaughter.

As the Union troops marched with precision onto the killing field, Robert E. Lee was moved to comment, "It is well that war is so terrible. We should grow too fond of it."

Francis Walker's history of the Union's II Corps observed that the assault failed "from the utter absence of anything like a plan of operations. The troops were thrown over the river in a sort of blind hope that so splendid an army, in such overpowering numbers, would somehow achieve a victory."

Lincoln would declare that Burnside at Fredericksburg had "snatched defeat from the jaws of victory." Shortly thereafter, Ambrose Burnside was relieved of command of the Army of the Potomac and sent to a quieter post in Ohio.

Amazingly, fifteen months later when U. S. Grant came to make his headquarters with the Army of the Potomac, who should he find resurrected and in command of the army's IX Corps but Ambrose Burnside.

Throughout Grant's Battle of the Wilderness, Burnside was of no appreciable help. In fact, it could be argued that the bloody Wilderness battle occurred because Grant had to stop his army in the dense forest in order to wait for Burnside's corps, assigned to guard the rear, to catch up.

At the end of July, Burnside made his last blunder.

Having pushed to Richmond and beyond, Grant laid siege to the Rebel capital. The armies of the blue and the gray settled in for an extended confrontation, staring at each other across fortifications, each daring the other to attack.

Burnside's corps contained a regiment of former Pennsylvania coal miners whose commander convinced Grant that his men could tunnel under the Confederate fortification, plant a huge explosive charge, and blow a gap in Richmond's defenses through which Union troops could advance.

The Army Corps of Engineers advised that a tunnel longer than 400 feet couldn't be dug because of the lack of air at the far end. The Pennsylvanians, however, used an old coal miner's trick to create circulation by building a fire at the open end of the tunnel and running a wooden pipe the length of the shaft. The fire drew stale air out of the tunnel, thus sucking fresh air into the far end of the tunnel through the wooden pipe.

It worked. The tunnel extended 511 feet. Once under the Confederate position, a 75-foot-long lateral gallery was dug, forming a "T."

Burnside chose an African-American division to lead the attack through the Confederate fortifications immediately after the explosion was set off in the tunnel.

Three days before the detonation, however, Grant overruled that decision. As he explained later to the Congressional Committee on the Conduct of the War, "It could then be said . . . that we were shoving these people ahead to get killed because we did not care anything about them. But that could not be said if we put white troops in front."

Burnside, confronted once again with an unexpected change in plans, remained true to form, unable to make a decision. Assembling his division commanders, he instructed them to *draw lots* to determine which division would lead the charge! Moreover, Burnside failed to arrange special training for the division that would lead the attack. The black soldiers had received such training, learning, for instance, that they were to go around the crater blown in the Rebel fortifications, not into it. The new lead division did not have the benefit of such training.

On the morning of July 30, 1864, a tremendous explosion was detonated in the tunnel, spewing dirt and rock into the air, creating a huge crater 170 feet long, 60 feet wide, and 30 feet deep right in the middle of the Confederate line.

Burnside's men charged through the gap—leaderless.

The lead division's commander, Brigadier General James Ledlie, a drunken coward, was hiding in a bombproof shelter behind Union lines, getting soused on rum purloined from the surgeon. In protest against the decision not to lead with the black troops, Burnside's two other division commanders refused to lead their men as well.

Leaderless, the troops charged down into the bomb crater only to discover that without ladders they could not scale the other side.

Without leaders and without instruction to go around the pit, the men poured into the deep depression. Soon 10,000 Union soldiers were jammed together in the thirty-foot-deep hole. They could not move forward because they had no ladders to climb out. They could not move backward because their comrades continued to pour into the crater like lemmings.

When the Confederates recovered from the blast, artillery poured down on the hapless Federal soldiers in the hole. Rebel riflemen ringed the crater, firing down at the trapped mass. It was like shooting fish in a barrel.

When Grant came forward and saw what had happened, he ordered Burnside to stop the advance and withdraw the troops. Yet Burnside, as at Antietam and Fredericksburg, stubbornly fed the slaughter for another three hours.

"It was the saddest affair I have witnessed in the war," Grant observed.

General George Meade, commander of the Army of the Potomac, wanted Burnside court-martialed for incompetence. Grant banished Burnside from the army by sending him home on extended leave.

Indomitable Courage
JOHN BELL HOOD

The antithesis of Ambrose Burnside was Confederate General John Bell Hood, a quiet, sad-eyed, bloodhound-faced hulk of a man. Commissioned a first lieutenant in the Confederate army in 1861, Hood, within three years, was a full general commanding the second-largest army of the Confederacy.

A leader of unbounded courage, Hood was given command of a brigade of Texans just before the Seven Days' Battles. He wasted no time writing the "Texas Brigade" and himself into the history books. At Gaines' Mill (see Lesson One), Hood led his men in the fiercest fighting of the entire seven days, providing a decisive breakthrough of a three-deep Union line.

By the Battle of Antietam (also Lesson One), Hood was commanding a division that was virtually destroyed while repulsing Union attacks on the Rebel left. Stonewall Jackson, under whom Hood served that day, was so impressed that he recommended him for promotion to major general. The normally undemonstrative Stonewall's report on Hood's performance positively glowed with praise: "[His] duties were discharged with such ability and zeal, as to command my admiration. I regard him as one of the most promising officers of the army."

At Gettysburg, Hood was directing the second day's attack on the Union southern flank (see Lesson Seven) when he was hit by a piece of exploding artillery shell. Hood was carried from the field, his left arm ruined. The leadership void caused by his injury stalled the Rebel assault just long enough to buy the precious minutes that, in the end, determined the outcome on Little Round Top.

A crippled left arm, however, did not stop John Bell Hood. He convalesced for two months and then went back to the field, his useless arm in a sling.

His division was shipped to Tennessee and joined General Braxton Bragg's Army of Tennessee in September 1863, just as the Battle of Chickamauga was erupting.

Newly arrived, Hood was ignorant of the terrain and the disposition of other forces. Nevertheless, his aggressiveness immediately led him to march his men across the Chickamauga Creek into the Union position, where they clashed with Wilder's Lightning Brigade (see Lesson Three) at day's end.

When morning broke on the twentieth, Hood was awaiting orders from Bragg. As the sound of battle came from all around him, Hood impatiently continued to wait. Finally, in midafternoon his aggressiveness could be restrained no longer.

Hood moved out toward the sound of the guns on his own authority. His timing was prescient. At that very moment, there briefly appeared a break in the Union line and Hood's men rushed in. They penetrated all the way to the Union headquarters, forcing the Federal commander to scamper to security before the Confederates were repulsed by a Union counter-attack.

The following day was a reprise for Hood's division. Their mid-morning advance discovered Union troops that had just pulled out from the position they were to assault. In a major screw-up, the Union commander had ordered a withdrawal of the troops holding an essential part of the Union line.

The result was a gaping hole into which the Confederates poured. Chaos ensued—the Union army suddenly found Confederates where they expected their comrades to be and the Rebels' advance was so unexpectedly swift that it rapidly became uncoordinated. To make matters worse, Hood's Texas Brigade—his first command and still a part of his division—was clad in blue! Some genius in Confederate supply had decided shortly after Gettysburg to issue new—blue—uniforms.

In the melee, fellow Confederates, believing their Texas comrades to be Yankees, began firing on them. When the Texans broke, Hood rode into their midst to rally them and was struck by a bullet, this time in the right leg. Again, with their leader down, the air went out of Hood's division.

Hood lost all but a stub of his right leg that night. As after his previous injury, however, Hood was soon back in the field.

Jefferson Davis promoted him to lieutenant general and gave him command of a corps in the Army of Tennessee under its new commander, General Joseph Johnston. In July 1864, Davis promoted Hood to full general and gave him command of the Army of Tennessee, replacing Johnston.

The courage of John Bell Hood's convictions was undiminished by his infirmities. The warhorse kept riding to the sound of the guns. But returning to the field was a bad decision for both Hood and Davis. Even this general's undaunted courage could not make up for his physical limitations.

His right leg gone and his left arm useless, Hood refused to use an ambulance for transportation; instead he was strapped into the saddle by aides. Consider the physical challenge of riding a horse and maintaining balance with one arm and one leg. The physical exertion required to remain erect must have sapped his strength. And the frustration must have chafed on this most bold and active of leaders. The pain of fighting to stay atop his mount for hours on end must have been severe, at a time when the Confederacy had few, if any, pain-relieving drugs.

"Courageous" somehow seems inadequate to describe how Hood, despite his afflictions, continued to lead. However, his courage had become tragic. A Civil War general had to be able to ride rapidly to where he was needed on the field, both to assess the situation and to exercise control. Hood's infirmities limited that ability.

A general must be clearheaded, despite the stress of battle. Hood's pain and physical exhaustion surely must have sapped him and his judgment.

His raw courage in trying to overcome the physical hardship and physiological stress of war cannot be underestimated. But John Bell Hood did not distinguish himself in the Army of Tennessee. His defense of Atlanta against Sherman failed. His subsequent assault on the Union Army of the Tennessee cost the Confederacy his army.

John Bell Hood remains, however, one of the Civil War's stellar examples of a leader possessed by the courage of his convictions. As a combat leader at the brigade and division level, he knew no equal.

Craig McCaw's Visionary Conviction

In 1994, Craig McCaw sold McCaw Communications, the nation's largest cellular telephone company, to AT&T for $11.5 billion. In the process, McCaw became the largest individual shareholder of AT&T stock. He was an exceedingly rich person, and not yet forty-five years old.

Soft-spoken, Craig McCaw reached that point because he had a clear vision of his goal and the courage to stick by his convictions, even through some of the darkest hours.

Craig McCaw's story started in adversity.

The death of his father, John Elroy McCaw, of a massive stroke in 1969 threw the family estate into chaos. The family chain of radio and television stations and other investments collapsed. The bank handling the estate withdrew, declaring it insolvent.

Craig's mother, who had served as her husband's accountant,

was forced to sell off the stations and other investments to satisfy claims from the IRS and creditors.

All that was left was a small cable television system serving several thousand subscribers in Centralia, Washington, which the elder McCaw had put in trust for his four sons. When he graduated from Stanford, Craig—who had been running the cable system from his dorm room—borrowed against its value and used the money to buy other small, remote cable systems.

During this period, Craig McCaw developed the business model that defined his future: buy a property with money leveraged off the cash flow of other properties, improve service, increase rates, cut costs, and generate new cash flow with which to start the leverage process all over again.

He also practiced a management style that empowered his subordinates. He dispatched bright, young Turks into small towns with offers to buy the cable systems. With full authority to make decisions, the McCaw people would negotiate a deal while competing buyers were still working through their corporate hierarchies, awaiting the necessary approvals.

In 1982, the Federal Communications Commission started granting licenses for a new radio service called "cellular telephone." Craig McCaw, who had been thinking about this new communications frontier for over a year, walked away with six licenses for the new service.

Today the promise of cellular seems self-evident. In 1982, however, even its developer, AT&T, estimated that by the year 2000 there would be only 900,000 subscribers. Craig McCaw, however, saw more. (In fact, two years before the turn of the century, cellular subscribership had exceeded AT&T's estimate by more than seventy times.)

The cellular business was a lot like the cable business—once you built the infrastructure, it was a cash flow generator, and that cash flow growth could be leveraged to buy more cellular properties.

Craig McCaw saw something else in the promise of cellular. It wasn't just a technology or even a financial play. Untethered communications appealed to something at the basic core of human nature.

One day, McCaw and I appeared together on a CNN program. He floored me by launching into a discussion of the sociohistoric significance of wireless communications.

From the time they discovered seeds, human beings have been enslaved to places, he explained. The cellular business was more than a radiotelephone business. It gave individuals the ability to break one of the physical ties that had defined their lives for eons.

McCaw envisioned a business that appealed to the basic need of humans to be free of bondage to places and things. As such, its social significance should not be overlooked.

"Do you know that Alexander Graham Bell used to put cotton in the bell of his phone so that he couldn't hear it?" McCaw said to me one day. "Bell wanted the phone to work for him, not to have his activity dictated by its ringing."

Craig McCaw saw a similar concept for the cellular phone. Rather than the wireline phone dictating where subscribers could use it, McCaw envisioned subscribers using the wireless phone anywhere they pleased.

Exhibiting the courage of his convictions, in 1986, at the height of the cable television explosion, Craig McCaw sold all his cable systems to then-Washington Redskins owner Jack Kent Cooke for $755 million, in order to invest the money in his wireless vision. He leveraged his cash with borrowed money, more than $1 billion of it raised by junk bond king Michael Milken.

In 1986, McCaw bought MCI's cellular and paging properties for $122 million. He promptly sold most of the paging assets for $75 million, giving him the cellular business at a bargain price of just over $6.00 per subscriber. Obviously, MCI shared neither

McCaw's vision nor his convictions about the future of wireless telephones.

With acquisitions from MCI and others, McCaw eventually pieced together a nationwide wireless phone network, becoming the largest cellular operator in the country. If he was to be the major national force, however, he needed wireless phone systems in New York and Los Angeles, two markets that thus far had eluded him.

The operator of a chain of TV stations, LIN Broadcasting, owned the New York and Los Angeles cellular systems that McCaw yearned to possess, as well as licenses in Houston and Dallas.

Quietly, McCaw began buying LIN stock. By 1989, LIN recognized that it was being secretly pursued and sought another bidder. BellSouth, the regional Bell telephone company in the southeastern states, with revenues thirty times greater than McCaw's, decided to try to add LIN to its cellular portfolio.

McCaw dared BellSouth to oppose his efforts to acquire LIN. He let it be known that nothing would stop him from achieving his goal. Craig McCaw would "bet the farm" and he challenged BellSouth to do the same.

In a move that was universally perceived as insane from a business standpoint, Craig McCaw bid $3.5 billion in mostly borrowed money for 51.9 percent of LIN. Since he was already carrying $2 billion in debt on a cellular empire that produced just $500 million in annual revenue, "insane" sounded about right.

BellSouth withdrew from the bidding, announcing that at those levels LIN was ridiculously overpriced. Craig McCaw, however, stood firm, demonstrating the strength of his conviction in a wireless future.

As cellular continued to blossom, becoming the fastest-growing consumer electronic product in history, there was sufficient cash flow to meet McCaw's heavy debt commitments. His crazy "overpayment" began to look brilliant.

In 1994, twelve years after receiving his first FCC licenses and five years after the much-derided LIN acquisition, Craig McCaw sold all 3.9 million of his cellular telephone subscribers to AT&T and began to pursue his "Next" vision.

Craig McCaw could have sat back and enjoyed the fruits of his labors. His AT&T dividends alone were worth tens of millions of dollars in annual income. Now he had the opportunity to slow down, to work on issues he cared passionately about, such as the environment. Now he had all the time in the world to fly his jet and his seaplane and to cruise on his yacht.

His risk-taking had paid off. Craig McCaw was not only wealthy beyond comprehension; he was universally hailed as a visionary. He was offered a seat on the board of AT&T, the company that had defined telecommunications for over a century. He declined.

Instead of resting on his laurels, enjoying his wealth, Craig McCaw gathered together a group of former associates and set out *again* to redefine the telecommunications business based on his evolving vision.

Investing in or starting a series of companies, most of which symbolically feature the word "Next" in their name, Craig McCaw set out to do it again.

McCaw showed not only the tenacious courage of Grant but also the kind of "lead from the front" attitude of Robert E. Lee and John Bell Hood.

Lee risked himself to such an extent that his troops cried out, "Lee to the rear!" McCaw risked his fortune and his reputation as a visionary in a highly visible effort to shape the future of communications.

I don't believe that Craig McCaw knows exactly what communications systems will be the growth services of the twenty-first century, or what technology will be demanded for their delivery.

There is one thing, however, about which I believe Craig Mc-

Caw is ultimately sure—the new services will require new distribution capacity, even the choice of multiple distribution capacities. He is determined to play a role in *all* those distribution systems.

Regardless of how technology and the marketplace develop, Craig McCaw will be a player.

For wireline phone services, McCaw formed Nextlink and targeted small businesses, a market he felt was under-served by the traditional phone companies.

For mobile wireless distribution, McCaw bought Nextel. Its product looks like a digital cellular phone, but uses a technology that allows fleet vehicles and worker groups to talk with each other simultaneously by touching a single button.

And just to make sure the rest of the world can enjoy McCaw's vision, too, Nextel has purchased the licenses for São Paulo, Buenos Aires, Manila, Tokyo, and other major world markets.

For wireless service to fixed locations, McCaw purchased LMDS (Local Multipoint Distribution Service) microwave licenses at a Federal auction and assigned them to a new company called Nextband.

Not only will Nextband compete with the landline telephone companies for high-speed point-to-point telecommunications but the technology also will be usable for hauling the calls of Nextlink and Nextel over heavy usage routes.

For high-speed fiber-optic communications, like that required for the Internet, McCaw formed Internext. With a $700 million investment, he now controls fiber-optic capacity covering 15,000 route miles.

In perhaps his greatest visionary reach, Craig McCaw convinced Bill Gates, chairman of Microsoft, to join him as an equal partner in launching an "Internet in the sky." The new company, Teledesic, will launch 288 low earth orbit satellites at a cost of $9 billion.

Gates frankly acknowledges that he never would have invested in Teledesic unless McCaw was involved.

"Craig is an amazing person," the Microsoft billionaire told *Fortune* magazine admiringly. "He thinks ahead of the pack and understands the communications business and where it's going better than anyone I know."

Because they orbit closer to the earth than traditional telecommunications satellites, less power is needed to send a signal to Teledesic's "birds," and they have a higher capacity.

In a manner similar to how the Internet passes data along a wire network today, Teledesic will relay from satellite to satellite digital data, sound, and pictures to reach every spot on earth, from populous cities to remote areas in developing nations.

It was only the latest iteration of the far-reaching concept Craig McCaw had expressed in the CNN studio years earlier—wireless communications fulfilling a basic human need to send and receive information without being forced to connect to the end of a wire.

So far, Teledesic has not only convinced the world's governments to allocate the necessary frequencies for the new service, it also has convinced Motorola and Boeing to invest and to make the equipment. Some critics have heaped the same kind of scorn on McCaw for committing so much money to such an untested idea as they heaped on him for "overpaying" for cellular licenses.

Craig McCaw, however, continues to exhibit the courage of his convictions and lead the telecommunications industry from the front. His troops are not shouting, "Craig to the rear!" And if they did, he wouldn't listen anyway.

Who am I ???

Marching Orders

At the heart of leadership lies conviction in who you are and what you are about.

Such conviction permits the identification of the next hill. It offers a vision of the beyond. Such conviction also provides an anchor with which to weather the inevitable storms.

There can be no victory without conviction.

Lesson Nine

If You Can't Win . . .
Change the Rules

Think anew

To hell with the rules! The "rules of the game" are historic artifacts, most often made by the victor, and used to maintain his position. To prevail against the old rules get rid of them.

Confederate Colonel John Singleton Mosby changed the rules with unconventional operations behind Union lines. Thousands of Union troops were kept from the front lines chasing his tiny band of cavalry.

To Union generals William Tecumseh Sherman and Philip Sheridan, ending the war meant changing the rules by ending the protection of civilians who helped to support the Southern war effort. In the Deep South and the Shenandoah Valley noncombatants became targets of military action and the tide was turned.

The Information Age is one huge re-formation of the rules. It was a new set of rules that enabled a utility lineman to invent cable television, and a biophysicist to develop the PalmPilot. The electronic era seems to be saying, "If it ain't broke . . . break it!"

The other guy wrote the old rules. Win by writing your own rules.

The Gray Ghost
COLONEL JOHN SINGLETON MOSBY

Every night during the winter and spring of 1863, Federal soldiers removed a section of the road planking on Chain Bridge, a main artery across the Potomac River between Union-occupied northern Virginia and the nation's capital. Despite control of the territory at both ends of the bridge, the Federals took the precaution out of fear that John Singleton Mosby and his band of Confederate Rangers would sneak into Washington and perhaps even capture the President.

Such concern was not far-fetched. Mosby was nicknamed the Gray Ghost for his apparition-like ability to appear without warning, attack, and then vanish.

While the Civil War saw many innovations—rifled gun barrels, use of railroads and the telegraph—those innovations were refinements on already-existing tactics. Trains could move men more quickly than horses, the telegraph facilitated faster communication than couriers, and rifled barrels allowed soldiers to hit targets more accurately at greater distances.

But these advancements did not change the underlying nineteenth-century Napoleonic tactics of war—masses of men clashing head-on until one side broke or retreated. The most radical innovation of the Civil War, therefore, was the introduction of warfare without lines, a war fought by small bands of men operating wherever they pleased—guerrilla tactics.

To offset its shortcomings in both men and supplies, the Confederates changed the rules. In April 1882, the Confederate Congress passed the Partisan Ranger Act authorizing the creation of roving guerrilla bands behind Union lines.

John Mosby became the leading practitioner of this new form of warfare in which small bands of rapidly moving troops would appear, strike, and then disappear.

Mosby's goal was to help the outnumbered armies of the Confederacy by keeping as many Federals as possible chasing fruitlessly after him and, thereby, off the front lines. If he could further disrupt Union communications and supplies, all the better.

"A small force moving with celerity and threatening many points in the line can neutralize a hundred times its own number," Mosby explained. He declared that a guerrilla's success "is not measured by the amount of property destroyed or the number of men killed or captured, but by the number he keeps watching."

In his *Memoirs,* Union General Philip Sheridan confirmed the value of Mosby's new rules. Because of Mosby, Sheridan wrote, he was forced to deplete his front line strength in order to protect his rear.

Union General Joseph Hooker told a similar story. During congressional testimony, Hooker reported that he had assigned 6,100 Federal cavalry troopers to pursue a mere 200 of Mosby's Rangers. Keeping more than 6,000 Federal soldiers tied down behind their own lines chasing ghosts meant 6,000 soldiers that Lee's outnumbered legions did not have to face on the battlefield.

John Singleton Mosby, a slight, sandy-haired lawyer, began the war as a cavalry private. Promoted to scout for Major General "Jeb" Stuart's cavalry, it was Mosby who discovered the route for Stuart's ride around McClellan during the Peninsula Campaign (see Lesson One).

As the Confederate army prepared to go into winter quarters in 1862, Stuart allowed Mosby to strike out on his own with an independent command. Commissioned the 43rd Battalion, Virginia Cavalry, the unit was universally known as Mosby's Rangers.

By the end of the war, Mosby had been commended in Robert E. Lee's reports more than any other Confederate officer. Since the Confederacy bestowed no honors or decorations, such recognition was its highest accolade.

The Horses Are a Real Loss

Mosby's new rules were a puzzlement to Union generals unable to wrap their tradition-bound minds around the concept of an enemy that didn't respect front lines. Union Brigadier General Percy Wyndham, one of Mosby's early victims, refused to recognize the military significance of what was happening. Mosby was a horse thief as far as he was concerned.

One of Mosby's first exploits set the tone for his new type of warfare. On the rainy night of March 8, 1863, Mosby and a mere twenty-nine of his men boldly rode through Union lines into Fairfax Court House, Virginia, the headquarters of several Union cavalry regiments. The encampment, about a dozen miles from the White House, was so far behind the Union lines it was thought secure.

Under the old rules, this security meant it was necessary to post only a few sentries. The light security, abetted by the drizzly weather that kept the Bluecoats under shelter and allowed the Rangers to wear nondescript rain ponchos over their gray uniforms, permitted the Confederate band to roam unmolested through the Union encampment for over an hour.

While one group went to the stables and herded the horses onto the main street, Mosby and another group went in search of Union brass. General Wyndham, author of the "horse thief" epithet, had left earlier that day for Washington. Brigadier General Edwin Stoughton, however, was in town. Mosby and a handful of his men rode to the house where Stoughton was sleeping.

Upon gaining access to the general's room, Mosby ripped back the general's bedcovers, lifted his nightshirt, and smacked him across the behind.

"General, did you ever hear of Mosby?" the Ranger asked.

"Yes, have you caught him?" Stoughton replied.

"He has caught you!" Mosby laughed.

The Union general, accompanied by thirty-two other Yankees and a herd of fifty-eight horses, was subsequently led back through the Union lines, prisoners of war.

That the enemy could operate with such impunity deep in Union-controlled territory so close to Washington shocked the nation. President Lincoln tried to put a good face on the event, quipping that he could create a new general in five minutes, but the horses were a real loss.

Mosby had changed the rules of engagement. Henceforth, the war was going to be fought everywhere, not just on the front lines.

Changing the Rules for Cavalry

Mosby was much more than a daring night raider, however. His Rangers were detached cavalry, engaging Union cavalry units in skirmishes behind the Federal lines. When these clashes occurred, Mosby changed the rules again to give his small band an advantage, even against larger forces.

U.S. Army doctrine of the time held that the saber was "the most deadly and effective weapon that could be placed in the hands of a horseman." As a result, at the war's outset, the Union army bought thousands of swords from France and Prussia.

Mosby discarded that doctrine. First of all, the noisy clanking of swords on mounted men, while romantic, was not conducive to stealthful approach by apparitions in gray. Moreover, the sword was utterly useless against the new, more accurate, rapid-firing weapons.

"My men were as little impressed by a body of cavalry charging them with drawn sabers as though they had been armed with cornstalks," Mosby scoffed. Instead of swords, the Rangers were outfitted with six-shot pistols and repeating carbines, usually captured from Union troops.

"My command reached the highest point of efficiency as cavalry," Mosby boasted, "because they were [each] well armed with two six-shooters and their charges combined the effect of fire and shock."

The engagement at Miskel's farm on April 1, 1863, was a classic example of Mosby's new rule of the sword against the six-shooter.

After a long ride the day before, Mosby and sixty-five or so of his Rangers bedded down in the barn of Tom and Lydia Miskel's farm, north of Leesburg, Virginia. Early in the morning, a Ranger who had stopped to spend the night with his family came riding across the fields, firing his pistol and shouting, "The Yankees are coming!"

Indeed, 150 men of the 1st Vermont Cavalry fell upon the unprepared Rangers. It was a perfect trap. The Rangers and their mounts were caught in the Miskels' barnyard, penned in by a high board fence, outnumbered better than two to one.

Union Captain Henry Flint had split his men into two groups. One squadron was arrayed at the farm gate to block any Rebel flight. The other squadron was sent forward to attack the Rangers trapped in the barnyard.

Flint was still operating under the old rules. In a fatal error he ordered a saber charge instead of having his men dismount and use their carbines.

By this time, approximately twenty Rangers were on their horses, many without saddles. Mosby ordered a charge. His men poured out of the barnyard, pistols blazing. Their feisty response stopped the Bluecoats. As more Rangers raced out of the barnyard, Mosby directed them to attack the Union cavalry.

The Federals gave way and fled—straight into their own rear

guard, Flint's reserve squadron and the barrier it had built to block the farm gate. Now it was the Union horsemen who were trapped. The Rangers' pistol fusillade overpowered the sword-waving Union troopers.

"They shot before sabers could strike," one account explained.

Mosby had, again, successfully demonstrated one of his new rules—a flailing saber was no match for a Ranger's revolver.

"I regret to be obliged to inform the commanding general that the forces sent out . . . missed so good an opportunity of capturing this Rebel guerrilla," wrote a Union officer in his report following the Miskel farm disaster. "It is only to be ascribed to the bad management on the part of the officers and the cowardice of the men."

Mosby's description of the action was more on point, "Unlike my adversaries, I was trammeled with no tradition that required me to use an obsolete weapon."

Mosby had changed the rules, again. As a result, he was winning.

Mosby's Confederacy

During the twenty-eight months of operations by Mosby's Rangers, the area from the outskirts of Washington to the Shenandoah Valley became known as "Mosby's Confederacy," despite the fact it was garrisoned throughout by Union troops.

The apparition-like quality of Mosby's force came from a simple concept—another of Mosby's new rules. Instead of maintaining garrisons, the Rangers lived with local sympathizers. Two or three Rangers would stay at a "safe house," often equipped with a trapdoor or secret panel which led to a hiding space in case of Union patrols. Upon a signal—say, Mrs. Edgar's quilt being hung out for air—the Rangers would assemble at a predetermined point, strike, and just as quickly disperse again.

"They had for us all the glamour of Robin Hood and his

merry men, all the courage and bravery of the ancient crusaders, the unexpectedness of benevolent pirates and the stealth of Indians," wrote a resident of Mosby's Confederacy.

Their opposition saw them differently, of course.

"Every farm house in this section was a refuge for guerrillas, and every farmer was an ally of Mosby, and every farmer's son was with him, or in the Confederate Army," complained a Massachusetts cavalryman stationed in Virginia.

The Union generals eventually determined that they, too, had to play by Mosby's new rules. Copying Mosby's innovations, Union cavalry eventually banished sabers to the parade ground and adopted tactics relying on the carbine and the six-shooter.

The Union army also struck at the Rangers' ability to hide among a sympathetic populace. If one secret of Mosby's success was his ability to disappear into and live off the landscape, the Union army would change that landscape.

In 1864, after a frustrating year of watching Mosby and his men disappear into thin air, the Union adopted a new scorched-earth policy in Mosby's Confederacy. Heretofore, the gentlemanly rules of war had avoided involving the civilian population. However, if that population was going to support Confederate combatants, then it would suffer the same consequences as the combatants.

Citizens suspected of harboring Mosby's men were summarily arrested and held. The entire population of northern Virginia was made to suffer as farms, mills, and any other facilities capable of sustaining Mosby's men were destroyed.

Nevertheless, Mosby fought on, continuing to evolve his tactics, to grow his forces, and bedevil Union troops. The Union generals, however, had finally caught on to the new rules and countered with some rule changes of their own. Mosby had been right—if you can't win by the old rules, change the rules—and his new rules had now become doctrine for both sides.

When the end came and Lee surrendered, Mosby flaunted the

rules one last time. Refusing to surrender, he simply disbanded the 43rd Battalion, Virginia Cavalry. One final time, Mosby's Rangers simply disappeared.

Total Destruction, 1864–65
GRANT INTRODUCES NEW RULES IN THE EAST

When Grant came east to take overall command of Union forces, he left his most trusted lieutenant, Major General William Tecumseh Sherman, in charge of the Federal troops in the Western Theater. Having campaigned together for two years, Grant was confident Sherman would do what was necessary to prevail.

The commanding general was much less sure of the leadership in the East, however, and so he made his headquarters with the Army of the Potomac.

Since First Manassas (Bull Run), Union forces in the East had run through six commanders, none capable of stopping the Confederates. Union activities in the East had developed into a pattern—a major engagement, usually a loss, followed by retreat, then a period spent licking the wounds in preparation for another battle and another likely loss.

Grant was determined to change the ultimate outcome by changing the old rules and establishing a new pattern of continuous fighting that would ultimately take its toll on the Rebels.

Under Grant, the Campaign of 1864 (see Lessons Two and Eight) was unlike any waged before in the East. The first forty or so days of that campaign, for instance, saw almost daily contact between the Union and Confederate forces. No more of the "engage and fall back" strategy of the past.

Under the old rules, the Union had been unable to win, in part because the smaller Rebel forces were allowed to regroup, resupply, and maneuver after each battle. Grant changed the rules to take advantage of the Union's superiority in men and matériel by decreeing constant engagement with the enemy.

The losses were horrific. In the first combat of the 1864 campaign, the Battle of the Wilderness, Grant lost more men than were lost in the battle and ignominious retreat at Chancellorsville thirteen months earlier. Grant's new rules, however, called not for retreat but rather for continued engagement with the enemy. Thus, after the Wilderness, Grant moved south in what was to become a pattern of movement and engagement, movement and engagement, that would fill the next six weeks.

Other Union commanders had started for Richmond only to be stopped after a single battle. Grant, although hit and hurt, changed the rules and kept moving—right to the door of the Confederate capital.

Sherman Changes the Rules

Changing the rules was nothing new for Ulysses S. Grant. As we have seen, his Vicksburg victory had resulted from abandoning traditional military doctrine and cutting loose from his base of supplies to live off the land as he attacked (see Lesson Two).

At the time, his most trusted lieutenant, William Tecumseh Sherman, had opposed such a move, warning that it violated the basic military axiom that an army must maintain a means of resupply. The victories at Jackson and Vicksburg, however, converted Sherman. He became a believer in independent, unsupported movement of an army.

Thus, the following year, after he had taken Atlanta, Sherman requested Grant's approval for a live-off-the-land campaign through the heart of the Confederacy—Georgia, South Carolina, and North Carolina. Grant was at first opposed to the plan, preferring Sherman to concentrate on Confederate General John Bell Hood's army, which after being chased from Atlanta, now lay between the Union forces and their base in Tennessee.

Finally, Grant relented. Hood would be left to the mercies of Union Major General George Thomas, while Sherman, with 62,000 men, would strike off through the South, unsupported.

Sherman's strategy was a reprise of Grant's at Vicksburg the preceding year. But "Cump" Sherman added some innovations of his own, specific to the course, duration, and objective of the campaign.

Sherman envisioned a military campaign conducted for political purposes. In a major change of the rules, Sherman's goal was not the destruction of the Rebel army, but the destruction of the Southern way of life.

"This may not be war, but rather statesmanship," Sherman wrote Grant in recognition of the political ends he sought.

"Taking a large army through the Confederacy would prove to distant Southerners, as well as to those in Sherman's path, that the North had the power to conquer the South," historian Charles Royster elaborated in *The Destructive War*.

It wasn't just Sherman's route that was significant, but also what happened along the route. Early in the war, Sherman had fought by the gentleman's code of conduct. Civilians and their property were to be respected. The only objective was the defeat of the enemy on the battlefield.

Out of a respect for humane behavior, and also to preserve discipline among the troops, civilians were not to be the direct targets of the war. Such a policy, it was felt, would also help build decent relationships with the conquered.

When plundering followed the Battle of First Manassas (Bull Run), Sherman scornfully wrote, "No Goths or Vandals ever had less respect for the lives & property of friends and foes, and henceforth we ought never to hope for any friends in Virginia."

In 1862, as troops under his command moved through Mississippi and Tennessee, Sherman saw to it that the army paid for supplies taken from local residents. Out of respect for property, he even refused to help slaves flee their masters.

By late 1863, however, the realities of the war had convinced Sherman that it was essential to change the rules.

"It is none of our business to protect a people that has sent all its youth, arms and horses, and all that is of any account to war against us," a less benevolent Sherman declared. "The people have done all harm they can, so let them reap the consequences."

As a part of those consequences, Sherman conducted a "scientific" advance from Atlanta. Using data from the 1860 census, he knew exactly what was in each Georgia county in his path— opportunities for resupplying his troops as well as targets for destruction.

Sherman's army assigned groups of soldiers to forage for provisions. Called "bummers" by their comrades, these units ranged through the Southern countryside confiscating everything in their path.

Livestock went directly to the commissary. Grain was accumulated until a mill was located where it was ground into meal for bread. As soon as that task was accomplished, the mill was demolished. Cities and farms were destroyed, homes as well as factories were burned, bridges were toppled, and railroad tracks became "Sherman Bow Ties"—the rails were ripped up, put atop a bonfire of burning ties until red hot, and then twisted around a tree.

Thus was cleared a path thirty to fifty miles wide from Atlanta to Savannah and then from Savannah into South and North Carolina.

In a major change in the rules, William Tecumseh Sherman brought a vengeful campaign against those Southerners who enabled and encouraged the Civil War.

"Three years ago by a little reflection and patience they could have had a hundred years of peace and prosperity," Sherman wrote in 1864. "Last year they could have saved their slaves, but now it is too late . . . Next year their lands will be taken . . . and in another year they may beg in vain for their lives."

Sheridan in the Shenandoah

While Sherman was leading the war in the west, Ulysses Grant tasked his other protégé, Major General Philip Sheridan, to do what had heretofore been impossible—clean Rebels out of the Shenandoah Valley, Virginia's breadbasket and the highway followed by every Confederate incursion into the North.

Grant had a simple vision of what needed to be done—apply Sherman's tactics to the Shenandoah Valley, while destroying the Confederate army that had long called the valley home.

The fertile fields that fed Lee's army and provided refuge for Mosby's Rangers should, Grant instructed, be turned into, "a barren waste . . . so that crows flying over it for the balance of this season will have to carry their provender with them."

But first, Confederate Major General Jubal Early and his troops had to be cleared from the valley, a task Union Major General David Hunter had been unable to accomplish.

Sheridan was the answer.

Grant wrote, "I want Sheridan put in charge of all the troops in the field with instructions to put himself south of the enemy, and follow him to the death."

Grant had changed the rules and pursued Robert E. Lee daily all the way to Richmond. Now Sheridan would apply the same fight-and-follow rules to the Rebels in the valley, pursuing Early's troops "to the death."

"This, I think, is exactly right," Lincoln wired his commander.

The campaign did not start with a flourish. For six weeks Sheridan and Early felt each other out and both Lincoln and Grant grew impatient.

The diminutive, scrappy "Little Phil" Sheridan, however, had a plan. On September 19, 1864, Sheridan's 37,000 Union troops attacked Early's 15,000 Rebels outside Winchester, Virginia. The victory went to Sheridan, despite his 5,000 casualties (against 4,000 casualties suffered by Early's troops).

Early retreated about twenty miles to high ground known as Fisher's Hill.

Only three days after the Winchester battle, Sheridan attacked again. Jubal Early was convinced his Rebels had a strong defensive position atop Fisher's Hill from which to withstand any assault. His guns commanded the principal Union approach and a stream that flowed right through the field of fire would slow any Federal attack.

Phil Sheridan did nothing to disabuse him of that assumption. However, "Little Phil" had no intention of using the obvious approach.

Keeping the Rebels busy with feigned attacks in their front, Sheridan sent troops who were familiar with operating in difficult terrain to work their way along the mountain paths to the Rebel left flank. The flankers' attack was a huge success and Early retreated sixty miles farther, taking refuge in the cover of the Blue Ridge Mountains.

Sheridan was driving the Confederates from the field, but he also needed to carry out Grant's other mandate to destroy the granary and livestock in the valley. Sheridan adopted the same new philosophy that Sherman was implementing farther south.

"The people must be left with nothing but their eyes to weep with over the war," Sheridan commanded.

His troops carried out the order with a vengeance. At the end of the first week of October, Sheridan reported to Grant that he had "destroyed over 2,000 barns filled with wheat, hay and farming implements; over seventy mills filled with flour and wheat; have driven in front of the army over 4,000 head of stock; and have killed and issued to the troops not less than 3,000 sheep."

The destruction was particularly acute in Mosby's Confederacy, where the Yankees knew they were destroying the underpinnings of the Rangers' support. The Union troops were especially frustrated by the Gray Ghost. In just the last month, Mosby's 200 men had killed, captured, or wounded over 1,000 Union soldiers and captured large stocks of Union supplies.

Sheridan asked Grant for another change in the rules—to permit reprisals against Mosby's men.

Grant agreed.

"When any of Mosby's men are caught, hang them without trial," he ordered.

Union Major General George A. Custer implemented the reprisal order in late September, hanging two and shooting four captured Rangers. The hanged Rangers were left swinging in their nooses, with a sign around their necks: "This will be the fate of Mosby and all his men."

If Sheridan was changing the rules of warfare, Mosby would do so also.

Despite the fact that another Ranger was subsequently caught and hanged, Mosby did not respond immediately. Over the next few weeks, as a result of his normal operations, Mosby captured hundreds of Union troops and sent them south as prisoners of war—except for those from Custer's command.

When he had twenty-seven of Custer's men, Mosby lined them up to draw lots. Seven would be executed in reprisal for the seven Rangers. When it turned out that one of those who drew the death slip was a young drummer boy, Mosby ordered his lot recast and those who had dodged fate once had to draw again.

The seven unlucky ones were taken off to be hanged or shot. Along the way two of them escaped. The executions of the others were carried out.

Immediately following Mosby's eye-for-an-eye executions, the Rebel sent a note to General Sheridan: "Hereafter, any prisoners falling into my hands will be treated with the kindness due to their condition, unless some new act of barbarity shall compel me reluctantly to adopt a line of policy repugnant to humanity."

The Union reprisals stopped.

The Confederates mounted one more attempt to push Sheridan out of the valley.

Lee reinforced Early, and "Old Jube" developed and executed a beautiful plan. On the night of October 18 through the morning of the nineteenth, four Rebel divisions silently moved into position to attack the left flank of the Union force camped close to Cedar Creek, about fifteen miles south of Winchester. General Sheridan was not present, having gone to Washington for two days of meetings.

At 5 A.M. the morning of the nineteenth, the Rebels attacked, the assault was a total surprise, and the Bluecoats were routed. By mid-morning, General Early was basking in a victory made even sweeter by the fact it was exactly one month to the day since his defeat at Winchester. However, Early did not follow Sheridan's example and press his advantage after the victory. Instead, he waited for the Bluecoats to withdraw, as had happened in the past. It was a fatal mistake.

General Sheridan's return from Washington had taken him to within about a dozen miles of the Cedar Creek encampment the night before. Awakened by the booming of artillery, he immediately rode to the firing and discovered his army in disarray.

Historian James McPherson describes Sheridan's action that day as "the most notable example of personal battlefield leadership in the war."

As his men cheered his arrival, Sheridan shouted, "God damn you, don't cheer me! If you love your country, come up to the front . . . Come up, God damn you! Come up!"

Sheridan wasn't about to play by the old rules. For most of the day, instead of withdrawing as Early expected, Sheridan re-formed his troops. Finally, at around 4 P.M., he counter-attacked. When the attackers discovered a weak spot in the Confederate line, Sheridan poured his men through it, yelling, "Run! Go after them! We've got the God-damnedest twist on them you ever saw!"

It was a "twist" all right. The counter-attack turned a splendid Confederate victory into a total rout.

Jubal Early's Rebels fell back once again to Fisher's Hill—whipped for the third time in thirty days by "Little Phil" Sheridan. The Rebels lost most of their artillery, all of their ambulances and ammunition wagons, and most of their forage wagons, along with almost 3,000 men. Their days as a major fighting force were over.

Phil Sheridan had implemented the new rules to perfection. The Rebel army was driven from the Shenandoah Valley and Lee's breadbasket was emptied. There would be no more incursions northward to threaten Washington.

Leadership Lessons in Business
JOHN WALSON AND JEFF HAWKINS

John Walson and Jeff Hawkins are about as different as any two individuals can be.

Walson was a utility lineman in the backwoods of Pennsylvania educated at the school of hard knocks. Hawkins, the son of an inventor, was an engineer who decided to get a Ph.D. studying the human brain.

John Walson and Jeff Hawkins, however, had an essential trait in common—when they couldn't win, they changed the rules. As a result, they each opened the door to a whole new technology.

The Birth of Cable Television

Cable television generates almost $31 billion in annual revenue, with the potential for much greater growth ahead from clear digital pictures, fast Internet connections, two-way interactive transmissions, and 500 channels of programming.

That the cable industry exists at all is attributable to John Walson, a part-time utility lineman and appliance store owner in the tiny town of Mahanoy City, Pennsylvania. In the late 1940s, John Walson decided to change the rules, and in the process, inadvertently invented cable television.

The post-World War II period saw the introduction of commercial television. But Mahanoy City, located about seventy-five miles northwest of Pittsburgh, was in a valley in the Appalachian Mountains. So its 10,000 residents could not fully enjoy the new medium that was taking the country by storm because the mountains surrounding their town interfered with the signals from TV stations in Pittsburgh and elsewhere.

The residents of Mahanoy City saw more "snow" than programs on the tiny black and white picture tubes of their new television sets—a problem for a television salesman like John Walson. In order to entice people to shell out $300 or more for a television set, Walson began taking customers to the top of one of the surrounding mountains where he would plug in the TV and get clear reception.

It was a hard sell, however, since few people lived high enough up the hill to experience clear reception.

On a historic June day in 1948, John Walson put his utility lineman experience to work. He climbed a seventy-foot utility pole atop one of the mountains surrounding Mahanoy City, attached a television antenna, and ran a wire from the antenna down the mountain, through the trees, to a TV set in the window of his appliance store.

Mahanoy City residents could suddenly see a clear television picture. Walson knew he was on to something when people started congregating in front of the store to watch their favorite programs.

John Walson had changed the rules for a simple, personal reason—to sell more television sets. But it soon became obvious that his innocent innovation would have a much more far-reaching impact when townspeople began asking if they could hook the TV sets in their homes to his mountaintop antenna.

For a $100 installation fee and $2.00 per month, John Walson offered the first cable television service.

As he added more and more new customers and created more and more branches off the main antenna line, the laws of physics began to work against Walson. He had to overcome the drop in signal strength caused by the length of the antenna lead by installing simple set-top signal boosters. And if Walson was going to offer a consumer service for which people paid, he had to overcome another pesky problem—whenever it rained, the antenna service went out.

Within a couple of years, Walson replaced the original antenna wire with coaxial cable, a copper core with shielding to contain the signal. Tube amplifiers, like those the telephone company used to boost voice signals as they traveled over the phone lines, were designed and built by hand to boost Mahanoy City's TV signals.

To know John Walson was to appreciate the magnitude of what he had done. Polished he was not. A technical genius he was not. Yet he realized he couldn't win unless he changed the rules that governed how people received their TV signals.

One day in the mid-1970s, John Walson showed up in the office of the National Cable Television Association, where I worked. Under his arm he carried what could only be described as a rusted tin can filled with ancient-looking radio tubes. He put it down on my desk.

"This is the first cable television amplifier," he explained.

With that rusted tin bucket, John Walson had changed the rules, inventing an industry that ultimately changed the way the world receives its information.

PalmPilot's Radical Change

The PalmPilot is the fastest-selling computer product ever. In its first eighteen months on the market, customers snapped up 1 million of the cleverly designed and incredibly useful handheld computers.

While other companies had invested an estimated $1 billion to develop a Personal Digital Assistant (PDA)—Apple, reportedly, responsible for half that amount with its ill-fated Newton—Jeff Hawkins produced his first working model PalmPilot on an investment of just $3 million.

Before Jeff Hawkins, the son of an eccentric inventor, could succeed, however, he had to fail. He ultimately succeeded because while he persevered, he also changed the rules.

In 1988, Hawkins left the University of California at Berkeley without the Ph.D. in biophysics he had pursued for three years. But Hawkins coupled his aborted doctoral study of how the brain recognizes patterns with his previous experience at Intel and GRiD Systems to develop computer code for handwriting recognition software. He called it PalmPrint.

PalmPrint became the software underpinning for the Zoomer PDA—a product bomb. Sold through Radio Shack, the Zoomer's $700 price tag was beyond the reach of most of the Radio Shack faithful. And it didn't offer much to justify the price. Loaded up with peripheral drivers and ports, the Zoomer was bulky and slow. The keyboard was far too small and the handwriting software was too primitive to be a reliable substitute.

The Zoomer came a cropper—but not before research among those who did buy one turned up a startling fact. Consumers didn't want the Zoomer to *replace* their PC; they wanted a handheld device to *supplement* their PC.

Hawkins took his basic software and started over again. The device he sought to create had to meet two criteria: it had to fit in a shirt pocket and its performance had to be fast and agile enough to recognize handwriting. His competition wasn't the computer; it was a pad of paper and a pen.

Removing all the ports, drivers, and other PC-like gizmos from the Zoomer would help him get his new device down to size. But the computing power necessary to recognize individual handwriting slowed performance and still wasn't reliable.

Then Jeff Hawkins changed the rules.

He and all the other PDA developers had been trying to teach a computer to think as fast and to recognize as many varieties of handwriting styles as the human brain. Why not go at it the other way? Why not teach humans to change the way they write in order to better communicate with the computer?

The idea was counter-intuitive. Hawkins was proposing to go against the direction of the entire computer fraternity. More than one person told him in those early days that he was nuts to try to change human behavior just to suit the limitations of a computer.

"People are smarter than appliances," Jeff Hawkins argued to the doubters. "They can learn. People like learning. People can learn to work with tools. Computers are tools. People like to learn how to use things that work."

Out of that concept came PalmPilot's Graffiti software. Graffiti provides users with an entirely new alphabet that eliminates all the cross strokes in letters—the times the pen comes off the page to complete a letter. It was these strokes that made it so difficult for earlier PDAs to recognize handwriting.

With this rule-breaking idea, Hawkins reduced the recognition complexity for the software. In the Graffiti alphabet, an "A," for instance, looks like an upside down "V,"—no cross stroke, no need to lift the pen thus adding confusing variations. Different hands may draw that inverted "V" differently, but the basic stroke is so simple that the computer can easily recognize it as an "A."

Millions of people have changed their handwriting in order to communicate with their PalmPilot. By changing the rules, Jeff Hawkins created a computer to replace paper and pen.

Marching Orders

As a young man, a mentor, George Koch, continually impressed on me that, "Doing things the way you did them last year is just an excuse for not thinking."

Successful leaders change the rules rather than let habit or the opposition define the contest.

Putting It All Together: The Lessons of Bill McGowan and MCI

Today it is hard to recall when there was *The* Phone Company and no competition for services.

More than any single person, Bill McGowan is responsible for today's competitive telecommunications landscape and its bounty of growth and innovation—not just for those companies engaged in telecommunications, but for all consumers worldwide.

"We're the phone company, we don't care," was the basis for comedienne Lily Tomlin's character Ernestine, the sneering and indifferent telephone company operator. The routine always got knowing laughs because it so accurately portrayed the reality of the pre-MCI marketplace.

McGowan's MCI broke the mold. As a result, more services were made available to more consumers at lower prices than ever before. What began as one company's challenge to The Phone Company set the stage for what has become a worldwide competitive revolution in telecommunications technology and service.

The Phone Company, however, was determined to crush McGowan's upstart. The battle made David versus Goliath look like an even match. MCI had only a few years to build a network equal to what the Bell System had put together over decades. Financially, MCI operated on a shoe-string.

And then there were the legal and regulatory hurdles. Over the years, AT&T had helped state and Federal regulators write rules to assure there would be only one telephone service provider. Now, AT&T, with the largest corporate law department in the country, counted on those rules to shut down MCI. At the Federal Communications Commission, in the courts, and before state regulators, AT&T used its clout and the arcane telecommunications laws to crush the competitor.

The story of MCI is the story of a corporate war in which each of the lessons of Civil War generals came into play to produce the ultimate victory.

MCI Battles AT&T

The Civil War reshaped the character of the nation. One hundred years later, MCI reshaped an essential component of that nation's economy.

Looking back to the late 1960s from today's perspective, the concept of *The* Telephone Company seems so foreign. The company that delivered local telephone service was also the company that provided long distance service and the company that manufactured the equipment to originate, transmit, and receive those services.

The Bell System of AT&T was a "natural monopoly," or so AT&T had taught everyone to believe.

Eleven years after the end of the Civil War, Alexander Graham Bell patented his "electric speaking telegraph" technology, better known as the telephone. Shortly afterward, multiple, rival companies offered local service.

Soon after the turn of the century, the manager of one of those companies, Theodore Vail, guided the acquisition of the independent local companies by long distance provider AT&T on grounds that telephone service could support only one integrated provider. Vail became the father of the monolithic Bell System.

The natural monopoly concept was a sweet deal for AT&T. In return for submitting to rate regulation (which guaranteed it a "fair" return), AT&T became the only long distance company as well as the sole provider of local service in the markets it chose to serve.

For the next half century, AT&T worked with Federal and

state governments to draw up the rules that assured its continued monopoly position.

The company's vigorous assertion of its monopoly rights knew no bounds. For instance, AT&T also owned the phone book business with its lucrative advertising. Arguing that the phone book was an essential component of its monopoly network, the company was able to shut down the distribution of independently produced vinyl covers for the phone books.

Ma Bell successfully argued that the advertising printed on the covers compromised the integrity of the natural monopoly and the benefits it provided society!

The downside of a monopoly is the absence of incentive to innovate. In the early 1960s, an Arkansas entrepreneur, Tom Carter, developed a device that allowed a two-way radio to be patched into the telephone network.

Defining the Carterphone as a "foreign attachment" to the network (i.e., equipment not manufactured by AT&T), the Bell System threatened to cut off service for anyone caught using the device. But, in a landmark 1968 decision, the Federal Communications Commission (FCC) ended AT&T's monopoly in telephone equipment by approving the Carterphone.

For the first time, a competitive breeze wafted through telecommunications.

In 1963, a few years before the Carterphone decision, an Illinois businessman, Jack Goeken, formed Microwave Communications, Inc. (MCI) and asked the FCC for permission to build a string of microwave relay stations along Route 66 from Chicago to St. Louis.

Goeken, whose occupation was selling two-way radios, reasoned that he could sell more of the devices to truckers if they could communicate with their home office via microwave relays when they were beyond the range of their radio's base station. Goeken also believed he could make money by selling the relay service to other communications users.

AT&T opposed the application.

The formidable AT&T legal apparatus—900 lawyers!—went to work to stop the Illinois upstart. Using the rules it had helped to develop over the years, AT&T threw up roadblocks at every turn. As a result, it was a full three years after Goeken's application before the FCC finally agreed to even hold a hearing on the subject.

By that time the start-up company was on the verge of going broke.

Searching for new capital, Jack Goeken found Bill McGowan. McGowan's drive and tenacity had taken him from jobs in the railroad yards to Harvard Business School and a stint on the business side of Hollywood. With Irish wit and bombast, and a twinkle in his eye, Bill McGowan had been successful enough as an entrepreneur that he didn't have to work unless he wanted to. He met Goeken through a mutual friend. Where Goeken saw a microwave network, McGowan saw a revolution. He purchased 25 percent of MCI for $35,000, the amount of the company's debt.

While Goeken did the technical work necessary to build the microwave network, McGowan raised the money to build it.

McGowan had a broader vision for MCI. In addition to relaying two-way radio messages between truckers and their home office, the network also would carry long distance telephone traffic for business customers in competition to AT&T. McGowan saw the opportunity to expand the Chicago-to-St. Louis model by building other facilities to serve customers across the nation—challenging Theodore Vail's fifty-year-old contention that AT&T was a "natural monopoly."

One year after McGowan joined the company, the FCC finally granted MCI its microwave licenses. The decision—on a close 4–3 vote—foreshadowed the regulatory fights yet to come.

Construction began in January 1971, seven years after Goeken's initial request to the FCC.

Twelve months and $4 million later, there were forty-four microwave towers, spaced approximately every twenty-five miles, along Route 66 from Chicago to St. Louis. Having overcome a half-century of established regulatory policy and the massive opposition of AT&T, MCI was a functioning reality.

With the successful FCC decision behind him and the first microwave route established, McGowan set out to expand the fledgling MCI network. Rather than risk amending the original license (which would give AT&T the opportunity to reopen the entire issue), McGowan formed seventeen new companies, each of which applied for a license for a separate new route—for instance, Chicago to New York. Money was raised to finance the expanded MCI by selling franchises to local investors.

"We eat guys like you"

Just because a Federal agency had voted in favor of competition, however, did not mean that AT&T would welcome rivals willingly. Although the FCC had ruled in 1971 that MCI had the right to connect callers on its microwave network with AT&T's telephone network, The Telephone Company decided to comply with the rule on its own terms.

In September 1972, AT&T told MCI that in order to interconnect, it would have to buy the necessary equipment with one lump sum payment and would have to pay AT&T for maintenance of the facilities. It was no secret that small, cash-strapped MCI could not meet those terms.

When McGowan sought a meeting with AT&T chairman John deButts to appeal, he got a full dose of The Telephone Company's scornful attitude toward the upstart.

After cooling his heels for three hours outside deButts' office, McGowan was ushered in to find the chairman behind his desk on the phone, with his back turned. For fifteen minutes McGowan sat there, ignored, reminded of his insignificance.

Finally, deButts hung up, swiveled his chair around, and

greeted McGowan with, "You know, we eat guys like you every day of the week."

"You're not going to swallow this guy," McGowan shot back.

At the time, MCI's gross annual revenues were less than $200,000.

Making Good on Promises

For the next dozen years both McGowan and deButts (and his successors) made good on their promises. AT&T worked mightily to stop MCI but Bill McGowan refused to be swallowed.

To pay for the build out of his nationwide network, McGowan raised money in the private market, the public market, and from vendors. Where it had taken AT&T decades to put a nationwide telephone backbone in place, MCI did it in one year.

McGowan was "Mr. Creativity" when it came to financing. To persuade his vendors to guarantee the loans he needed to buy their equipment, he agreed to let them increase their price by 50 percent to offset the risk. Paychecks were distributed to employees late Friday, after the banks had closed, thus allowing McGowan the weekend to cover the obligations. Equity funding was too expensive: Bill McGowan financed everything.

"I'd lease the wallpaper if they'd let me," he once told me.

All the while, AT&T continued to thwart the interconnection of calls on MCI's network with the Bell System's local affiliates. Ma Bell knew that by delaying interconnection it was delaying revenue to MCI—a double-barreled assault which reduced the funds MCI needed for operations and network construction, and made it harder for McGowan to raise capital to cover the shortfall.

The strategy was working. By the end of 1973, MCI was generating only about $100,000 per month in revenue, roughly one twentieth its monthly cash requirement. The more AT&T dragged its feet on interconnection, the more it could speed MCI's demise.

Bill McGowan had filed suit in court earlier to force AT&T to give him interconnection. Finally, in December 1973, the U.S. District Court in Philadelphia ruled in the case, ordering AT&T to provide interconnection at just and reasonable rates. It was a huge victory for MCI.

While AT&T complied, it also appealed the decision. When the appeals court reversed the lower court's order on the grounds it had usurped a regulatory role reserved for the FCC, AT&T wasted no time in striking back. The following day the connections of some key MCI customers were cut—often in mid-sentence.

AT&T had sent a message to potential MCI customers—do business with the upstart at your own risk.

Flank Attack

At about this point in time, I became a soldier in Bill McGowan's army.

The cable television industry, whose trade association I was heading, had its own problems with AT&T. Just as Ma Bell didn't like MCI's competitive microwave system, it didn't like the thought of the cable companies running another set of wires into America's homes—especially wires that had greater capacity than theirs.

The cable industry had its own litany of telephone company abuses and was looking for allies. Bill McGowan was the toughest, most tenacious potential ally on the block.

Both the cable industry and MCI wanted to offer services which competed with AT&T. Only the government, however, could force AT&T to stop its predatory practices and give the upstarts a fighting chance. Bill McGowan recognized that his future was in the hands of the policy makers and that he was only just beginning the battles of the courtroom and the hearing room.

"MCI is a law firm masquerading as a company," McGowan joked to me at the time.

While MCI struggled with financing, sales, and interconnection, McGowan issued orders to his "law firm" to launch a flank attack—the aggressive use of governmental remedies beyond the FCC. MCI supplied the U.S. Department of Justice's Antitrust Division with evidence of AT&T's alleged anticompetitive behavior. The Justice Department, sufficiently interested, subpoenaed documents and records from AT&T.

In September 1974, MCI filed its own antitrust suit against AT&T, supported by the same list of abuses it had turned over to the Justice Department. MCI sought damages for alleged violations of the Sherman Antitrust Act.

Finally, McGowan took his case to Congress. He proposed that Ma Bell be broken up into a local service company and a separate long distance company.

The Battle Rages

The flank attack would take time to develop. Meanwhile, MCI needed revenue badly. The original "private line" services connecting spread-out corporate facilities with voice and data transmission—the business that had grown out of those Route 66 microwave relay towers—was not generating sufficient revenue to fund McGowan's vision.

Burt Roberts, McGowan's vice president of operations at the time, developed a plan called Execunet, which allowed a user not connected to the MCI private network to dial a series of numbers on any phone to access MCI's service. Once on MCI, the customer would dial an authorization code and the number being called. The MCI network would deliver the call at a discount from AT&T's prices.

After a rocky start in the Washington, D.C., market, Execunet was launched to great success in Texas in January 1975. The manager of the Texas markets, Jerry Taylor, hired telephone solicitors to cold call small and medium businesses and tell them how they could save money on long distance with Execunet.

Within two months the service was profitable. MCI had its new revenue stream.

AT&T, of course, cried foul and petitioned the FCC to stop MCI from offering Execunet. In July 1975, the FCC agreed with AT&T and ordered MCI to cease Execunet service. Once again, Bill McGowan's "law firm masquerading as a company" looked to the courts for salvation.

The U. S. Court of Appeals, while not deciding the matter, stayed the FCC's order pending a final decision on the matter. Execunet's life-sustaining revenue continued. Before the issue was finally resolved in MCI's favor two years later, Bill McGowan's "law firm" would take the matter back to the FCC (where it lost) and through the court system all the way to ultimate victory in the Supreme Court.

Going After the Consumer Market

It was now time for Bill McGowan to take on AT&T in the residential market. The business services had worked because of the corporate mandate to increase profits by driving down costs. Whether Mr. and Mrs. America would go for the same option for their long distance calls from home was anybody's guess.

McGowan turned to the pioneer marketer of Execunet, Jerry Taylor, to oversee the new venture. A six-month test was designed, starting in Denver.

MCI's residential long distance service would be sold on television like Ginzu Steak Knives, with creative commercials that included a number to call to sign up. In March 1980, Denver television stations began carrying snappy, irreverent ads comparing the higher cost of an AT&T long distance call with the lower price of a call on MCI.

The phones at MCI rang off the hook. On the first day, the

response was so great it overwhelmed the order-taking capability. At one point, according to legend, the supply of customer order forms was exhausted and the phone representatives began writing order information on the wall with anything available, including lipstick.

Then the phones went dead. The day following the launch of MCI's residential service, callers trying to sign up were greeted with a recorded message announcing that MCI's number was no longer in service.

In what was described as an "accident," AT&T's local company, Mountain Bell, had disconnected MCI's phones.

MCI, however, had proved its point. Competition had come to the consumer market. MCI immediately accelerated its introduction of residential service into other markets.

For generations, long distance had been an expensive service used by average Americans only in emergencies or on special occasions. MCI's lower prices made it possible for anyone to pick up the phone to say in touch. Long distance personal communications would never be the same.

One day over breakfast, Bill McGowan commented, "The only sad thing about making long distance so affordable is that people are going to lose the skill of written communications, and the history it creates."

It All Comes Together

In the spring of 1980, during the same period as the successful launch of residential long distance service, a jury in Chicago decided the antitrust suit MCI had filed six years earlier.

It found AT&T guilty. After the treble damage calculation permitted by antitrust law, MCI was awarded $1.8 billion—the largest award of its kind in history. Through years of appeals, AT&T eventually reduced the award. But MCI gained new credibility while AT&T was losing credibility.

The stars were beginning to align for Bill McGowan and his

valiant colleagues in the telephone wars. By late 1981, MCI was signing up residential customers at the rate of 10,000 a month.

At the shareholders meeting that year, McGowan's Irish wit proclaimed that the letters "MCI" now stood for "Money Coming In."

Congress also was beginning to hear the pleas of McGowan and other telecommunications insurgents and was considering legislation to change telecommunications law to embrace competition.

Then on January 8, 1982, the Department of Justice made the bombshell announcement that it had settled its antitrust suit against AT&T with the agreement that Ma Bell would be broken up. The new telephone structure would be similar to what Bill McGowan had proposed years before—the separation of AT&T's long distance service from local service.

As part of the settlement, all long distance customers of AT&T would be given the opportunity to select which company they wanted for their long distance carrier.

Bill McGowan had won.

Fourteen years after the hard-driving Irishman with the glint in his eye joined a flat broke microwave relay company, the telecommunications market had been changed forever—thanks largely to his efforts.

Bill McGowan and Civil War Generals

I believe that Bill McGowan would have been a superb Civil War general. His leadership of MCI embraced *all* the lessons of the Civil War generals discussed in this book. Here's what I mean.

Lesson 1: Risk

The early battles between MCI and AT&T were strikingly similar to the battles between Robert E. Lee and George B. McClellan. Bill McGowan, like Lee, was a risk-taker. The entire AT&T culture, on the other hand, was built upon McClellan-esque risk avoidance.

McGowan's MCI repeatedly risked failure in the pursuit of victory. It was built on a willingness to tackle not only one of the world's largest corporations, but also the regulatory structure created to assure AT&T's "natural monopoly." To AT&T such risk was a foreign and unwelcome country.

Lesson 2: Tenacity

Recognizing that delay was deadly for its cash-strapped challenger, AT&T fought even the smallest pro-competition regulatory initiative by MCI.

When the legal niceties were exhausted, AT&T turned to less subtle, more direct obstruction. By cutting off MCI customers after one court decision and "accidentally" disconnecting MCI's connection with its customers, AT&T was willing to do whatever it took to thwart MCI.

But Bill McGowan, like Ulysses S. Grant 100 years before, refused to concede defeat and battled on relentlessly. Despite devastating delays, setbacks, and legal hurdles, Bill McGowan pressed on to victory.

Lesson 3: Embrace Change

At the center of the MCI story is change. MCI embraced change; AT&T resisted it.

MCI began with an entrepreneur's idea for changing communications between a business and its employees. AT&T's response was to oppose that innovation and all those that followed.

Theodore Vail, the father of the Bell System, by successfully selling the idea of AT&T's "natural monopoly" drove out all competition. And without competition, there is no pressure from the marketplace to change or innovate. AT&T attempted to have competition declared illegal instead of supporting the evolution of technology and of the marketplace.

As a result, AT&T clung to the old way of doing things, thereby stifling the evolution of technology. Ultimately, as the corporate battlefield changed around it and new technology changed the marketplace, AT&T kept on doing things the same as always. As a result, like Lee at Gettysburg, who couldn't adapt to the new advance in weaponry, it lost.

Lesson 4: Vision

To Bill McGowan the original MCI created by Jack Goeken was not just a string of microwave relay towers to retransmit the two-way radio signals of truckers—it was a private line telephone service waiting to happen to carry voice and data traffic between the facilities of major corporations. Bill McGowan was always seeking the next hill. The private line service eventually became a substitute for small and medium companies to AT&T's long distance service. From long distance for business customers, McGowan's vision expanded still further to long distance for residential customers.

From the beginning, Bill McGowan had a vision of what MCI could be.

Lesson 5: Audacity

Not only was Bill McGowan's vision audacious, the methods he chose to implement that vision were equally audacious. Like the great Civil War generals, Bill McGowan frequently defied common wisdom.

In challenging AT&T's historic "natural monopoly" in the market, McGowan launched a crusade to break up the Bell System. It was one thing to nip at The Telephone Company's heels. To go for the behemoth's jugular, however, at the very moment

Ma Bell was cutting off his cash flow, was nothing less than inspired.

The competitive restructuring of the American telecommunications market that resulted could not have occurred under AT&T's "business as usual, control the risks" mentality. Only through Bill McGowan's bold leadership was the breakthrough achieved.

Lesson 6: Use of Information

Bill McGowan did not suffer from George McClellan's hesitation in acting on crucial information. MCI was inventing a business, and any new information was put to work immediately. For example, MCI's test of residential long distance service in Denver was intended to run six months. The first week's results, however, gave McGowan all the information he needed—there were a lot of competitive service customers who would sign up for a low-cost alternative to AT&T. Within a week, service was launched in Cincinnati and launch plans in other cities were accelerated.

To exploit this new information, McGowan shifted MCI from the direct sales strategy used to sell business accounts to a television campaign aimed directly at consumers. The creative, irreverent commercials convinced consumers of the new reality in telecommunications competition long before the six-month test period had expired.

Lesson 7: Empowerment

The Civil War was fought by leaders who had never before led masses of men in battle. MCI was built by leaders who had never before run a telephone company. But Bill McGowan chose his subordinates well, expected them to deliver, and allowed them to do so.

AT&T practiced the antithesis of empowerment. With more employees than the U.S. Army had in Europe at the height of the

Second World War, AT&T was overstaffed, rigid, hierarchical. Employees did their jobs, nothing more. Independent action, with its potential for mistakes, was frowned upon.

MCI not only encouraged—but *required*—its people to take independent action.

Jerry Taylor, head of MCI Network, explained in the book *MCI: Failure Is Not an Option,* "I think what works best is to let people make some mistakes. Those who don't make decisions create the biggest problems for you, not the ones who make decisions and make mistakes."

One MCI employee quoted in the book said, "I actually heard Jerry say to people, 'You're not making enough mistakes.' "

Lesson 8: Courage of Conviction

Revolutionaries usually wind up as heroes . . . or hanged. It's impossible to lead the kind of revolution McGowan and his team did without an ample supply of conviction and the courage to see it through to the end.

"It's not just a job. It's me," was how Bill McGowan expressed his convictions to *Business Week.*

The other leaders of MCI reflected similar conviction. They all possessed the courage to leave responsible jobs and take significant salary reductions to test an unproven competitive theory against one of the largest and most powerful corporations in the world.

The MCI revolutionaries, throughout the battle, continued to up the ante on their convictions. MCI didn't remain just a relay service, it became a private line carrier, then a business long distance service, and then a residential long distance service. At each juncture, as MCI ratcheted up its attack on the Bell System, it faced the very real potential that it might lose everything.

But MCI—starting with Bill McGowan—had the courage of its convictions. The MCI team kept pushing forward, regardless of how daunting the task, or how bleak the outlook.

At the time it launched Execunet, MCI had been profitless for a dozen years. The company was loaded down with over $70 million in debt. And shortly after Execunet was launched, AT&T convinced the FCC to prohibit MCI from offering the new service. Yet the MCI team persevered and on the strength of a court stay (not a final decision, just a delay) they continued to sell Execunet, build their network, and raise the necessary capital to keep going.

It was a demonstration of conviction U. S. Grant would have admired.

Lesson 9: Change the Rules

The very existence of MCI represented a radical change in the rules.

Jack Goeken couldn't succeed at selling his two-way radios to truckers on Route 66 because of limited range, so he changed the rules for that business by building microwave relay towers, thereby expanding the reach of his radios.

To fulfill his vision of competing with AT&T, Bill McGowan further changed the rules, creating separate companies to apply to the FCC for microwave licenses in separate markets, rather than seeking to expand service by modifying MCI's original Route 66 license. MCI's growth would be paid for the same way McDonald's grew, with capital from local investors.

McGowan also changed the traditional buyer-seller relationship with equipment vendors. If a manufacturer wanted to do business with MCI, it had to guarantee the loan used to purchase the equipment. And McGowan was willing to allow them a 50 percent price increase in return.

McGowan changed the traditional role of the CEO by becoming a lobbyist . . . and a very adroit one. Public policy—the decisions of legislators, regulators, and judges—was as important to MCI's development as the more traditional corporate activities of finance, operations, and sales.

McGowan moved MCI's headquarters from Chicago to Washington, D.C., around the corner from the FCC.

"I want those FCC people to see a big MCI sign on the building whenever they come to or go from work," he explained to me.

Before MCI, The Telephone Company was a mere order-taker. Where else were residential and business customers going to go for telephone service or equipment?

MCI changed that rule, too, bringing up-to-date product sales and marketing techniques to telecommunications. To sell Execunet, MCI's salespeople literally ripped sections out of the Yellow Pages and began cold calling. The biggest change, however, came when television advertising made residential long distance service a consumer product to be sold just like soap or soft drinks.

Because MCI *was* change, its survival required that time and again it leaders had to change the rules.

Marching Orders

Corporate battlefield victories have, at their core, the same leadership qualities as victories on the military battlefield.

Leadership is timeless. The basic attributes of a great leader are as clear today as they were during the Civil War, as Bill McGowan proved.

Index

ABOUT THE AUTHOR

TOM WHEELER is the president of the Cellular Telecommunications Industry Association and the former president of the National Cable Television Association. He previously founded and ran telecommunications companies. He has had up-close involvement in the telecommunications and information revolution for over twenty years. During this period, he has worked closely with many leaders, both in business and government, an experience that shaped the observations in this book.